SHE CHALLENGED GOD AND GOD RESCUED HER

She Challenged God And God Rescued Her

Naylee Bartlett

Pinsan Books

ISBN: 978-0-9956823-2-0

CONTENTS

	Introduction	7
1	Supernatural Faith	9
2	Do Not Limit God By Your Unbelief	20
3	The Power Of Forgiveness	29
4	She Challenged God, And God Rescued Her	42
5	Caty's Testimony	56
6	Healing	60
7	Children Are Precious Gifts From God	65
8	My Teenage Years	69
9	Dreams And Visions	75
10	This Time My Dream Becomes Reality	86
11	Once Saved Always Saved	92
12	Remembering The Lord Jesus' Sacrifice	124
13	Do You Know Where Your Spirit Is Going To When You Die?	135
14	Did You Know God Has A Sense Of Humour?	145

INTRODUCTION

Life is void without God, for life itself comes from God—that's a fact no matter what you believe. For everyone knows there's a beginning and end of life and that life and death are ordained by God. Our life would not exist without a Creator!

Our life is like a book or a history where there is a beginning—when you were born, a middle part—when you got a job, fell in love, got married and have a family of your own, and then the end—when you say your final goodbye. And we all have experiences we learned in life. Some are bad, and we struggle and some are good, and we succeed; and during these stages in life some people experience the supernatural power of God.

And two of the stories I'm sharing here with you are supernatural experiences that compelled two young ladies to believe the Supernatural Power of God reached down to them and met them where they needed God most.

And I'm sharing this book with those who want to have a supernatural encounter with God.

1

SUPERNATURAL FAITH

Let me tell you, first of all, that everything comes from God, including our intelligence. He gifted us to use it in proportion to the ability we have received from Him. It says in Deuteronomy 8:18: ...***but remember the Lord your God, for it is He who gives you the ability to produce wealth.*** This ability we have works in conjunction with our needs. When God created man, he didn't need any medicine; he was perfectly fine and didn't need anything in the place where God put him, eastward in the Garden of Eden. Only after he was incredibly deceived (by exercising his freewill) did he feel the need of the presence of God in his life. Before that, he had free access to God's eternal presence. He led a contented life in God's garden. But immediately after Adam and Eve's natural physical senses were awakened, illness came to man's body. That's the fruit of disobedience and of knowing good and evil!

In the last book of the New Testament it says in Revelation 22:1–5 that there's a tree of life, which is at the centre of the city, and the leaves of the tree are for healing of the nations. God provided us with natural medicine. But the Lord Jesus' death and resurrection is His Supernatural provision, that by His stripes you are healed. He didn't just die and that was it, but He was resurrected back to life; not just the natural life now, but Supernatural life. He could pass through walls and locked doors, and eat breakfast with His disciples after His resurrection—see John 20:19–29 and John 21:5–12.

He didn't do that when He was in the physical body, with His disciples; it was only after He had been resurrected in His new body.

Above all things, all powers belong to God. We only have access to God's power when we walk according to His ways and will. Yes, we have power and freedom to exercise what we can already do. But we do not have an ounce of power (talking spiritually) without the Lord Jesus and God's Holy Spirit leading us. We would only have 'self-acclaimed' faith; maybe boasting of what we can do, when actually, the Lord God does it through us, when He blesses people. But He also cultivated wisdom in the heart of man (not ego) by giving us all ability, so we can all earn a living, as it is stated in Deuteronomy 8:17 & 18.

Now let us delve into supernatural faith. Some people experience miracles because they believe in the Supernatural power of God.

Supernatural faith is based not on your circumstances or on your own ability or experiences in the past, not even in the natural things you know of, but rather on Him (God), whom you anchor your hope with. For some people, just believing that there is God is a miracle on its own. But even for some of those older Christians who are well rooted in their past experiences, sometimes it's still a miracle for them to raise up their expectations that God heals today. Especially true of those who claim to be Christians but they believe miracles only happened when the Lord Jesus was here on earth and have now ended. Some Christians stop believing the works of the Holy Spirit too. That too is a miracle on its own for some Christians who call themselves well rooted in reading and hearing the Bible verses, and never put what they've known and heard and read into action. Their belief in the Lord's death and resurrection has become futile, just head knowledge. But the Lord Jesus rose (He didn't remain dead) and commanded His disciples to cast out the devil and heal the sick. This is now the spiritual—a Supernatural power of God through us the doers of His Word. We are in the flesh so we touch and minister to people in the flesh. The Lord Jesus left the work to us, as God the Holy Spirit could not just touch the people—who are not spiritually discerned (God is Spirit).

I didn't experience the Holy Spirit when I was in the Roman Catholic religion. I experienced God's power when I started putting into practice what I believed about what God's power could do through me. I'm only the vessel or the channel people tune into when I tell them about God's power that could work in them. Those who do not believe in the Holy Spirit cannot put into practice what they have heard, so God's word has no power in their own lives. Their faith is dead, buried in the coffin of their useless knowledge. As it says, ***faith without action is dead***, so knowledge without action is also dead—*kaput*, lifeless.

Supernatural faith is a deeper kind of faith that doesn't focus on yourself at all, or the spiritual gifts you think you have—not even on the anointing you're operating in, or the person who prayed for you when you got better—but fully on the Lord Jesus' sacrifice. So that you may give God the praise He deserves, your focus should be on the One who is bigger and higher than you and me. The Holy Spirt, whom the Lord Jesus sent for all believers to be their guide, He is The Power behind all Powers that we believers experience and encounter.

There is true power in the Name of Jesus Christ of Nazareth. It says in Philippians 2:10: ***That at the name of Jesus every knee should bow, in heaven and on earth and under the earth.***

Your supernatural faith means you put your

expectation outside of yourself and not on other people. It means you place your whole focus and expectation on God; who is higher and bigger than anything else in this world. He is the Creator of all things that exist today. When you put your whole trust in God, you will experience the Supernatural power of God in your life.

The trouble is all of us are affected with what we hear and see in the natural—it's human nature. But as a Christian, you must go deeper and higher than the natural, if you consider yourself a Christian believer. It's a sin just to expect or experience the natural, because it's no longer faith if it just works as it normally does! If we consider just the natural, it isn't faith anymore. Why? Because it is then just as ordinary as a non-believer's experience and belief! What makes you different from the Atheist, or the next-door neighbour who hasn't got faith in anything but nature? Nothing!

I don't think you can remain unchanged when you have encountered God's Holy Spirit. It's a sin if you're not willing to cooperate with the Holy Spirit's leading. He always enlarges your spirit man. For in Him there's always something new; He is not a stagnant God, He is God of multiplication, a God of changes and a God of new heights. It's no longer faith if you remain the same as you were, before you encountered Him. It says in Hebrews 11:6: ***And without faith it is impossible to please God, because anyone who comes to Him must believe that He exists and that He rewards those who earnestly seek Him.*** So we should earnestly seek God to experience His miracles and healing because that's the 'Nature of God'. It's Supernatural to us, but not to God as that is His nature—Super Natural. In fact, He truly expects us to believe in Him Supernaturally and the power of His Might.

In Mark 9:23, talking to the father of the sick boy,

Jesus said, *"'If you can'? Everything is possible for one who believes."* (Please read Mark 9:14–29.) The Word of God accomplishes everything He has said. That's why the Lord Jesus doesn't speak much, because He can create things by His own word alone. Supernatural faith comes from Biblical belief through personal relationship with the Lord Jesus and the Holy Spirit. When the Holy Spirit reveals anything to you, you have the licence to dig deeper through God's Word and work; His Hand will move by the faith you have received from Him. You can rest assured that God's hands will move when you're most expecting it. Unbelief stops the Lord Jesus' moving. He stopped healing people in His hometown because of their unbelief and unrepentant heart. ***He was amazed at their lack of faith***, see Mark 6:4–6 and Matthew 11:20. His goodness is not based on our faith alone, but also based on our personal relationship with Him. When you acknowledge God's revelations; you will experience God's power in your own personal walk with Him.

Supernatural faith has the freedom to impose on your circumstances what you know God will do; His supernatural power is not based on your feelings, situation, conditions or whatever is in front of you, which is always a better result than what you can see in the natural. Because when you know deeper in your soul that you have placed your true hope and deeper faith in an Omnipotent, Omniscient, and Omnipresent God, who knows no bounds, and holds no regrets to give you what you're asking for, you'll have what you ask of Him—see Mark 11:24. For as it says in Hebrews 11:1, ***Faith is the substance of things hoped for*** (your hope must come from your personal relationship with the Lord Jesus, His love for you)***, the evidence of things not seen.*** Supernatural faith is unseen, with deeper conviction from your very soul, through your faith in God, the Lord Jesus, and the work of the Holy Spirit.

If you believe and do not put what you know into practice, then it's useless for you and other people around you; it's no longer real faith, because it works just the way you expect it—nothing less, nothing more. It's just a belief system that fails from time to time.

These are a few examples that God is Supernatural in nature:

1. Supernatural faith brings an extra dimension to people's spiritual life. **Like when Elisha threw the stick on the water to make the head of an iron axe float**, it came up to the surface of the water—which is impossible in the natural to happen, but through Elisha's faith in God, He experienced God's creative power and made the impossible, in human terms, possible with those people standing with him. They experienced God's nature (an iron axe head floating in the water, a supernatural experience even to some of them, I believe, and to us) which was written for us as our guidelines in life, that we may also experience God's miracles as the old prophets did in the past. See 2 Kings 6:6.

2. And in 2 Kings 4: 1–7: *The wife of a man from the company of the prophets cried out to Elisha, "Your servant my husband is dead, and you know that he revered the LORD. But now his creditor is coming to take my two boys as his slaves". Elisha replied to her, "How can I help you? Tell me what do you have in your house?"* ***"Your servant has nothing there at all,"*** *she said,* ***"except a small jar of olive oil."*** *Elisha said,* ***"Go round and ask all your neighbours for empty jars. Don't ask for just a few."*** *Then go inside and shut the*

door behind you and your sons. Pour oil into all the jars, and as each is filled, put in into one side." She left him and shut the door behind her and her sons. They bought the jars to her and ***she kept pouring. When all the jars were full****, she said to her son, "Bring me another one." But he replied, "There is not a jar left."* ***Then the oil stopped flowing.*** *She went and told the man of God, and he said, "Go, sell the oil and pay your debts. You and your sons can live on what is left."* So she put her faith into action at the command of Elisha—by pouring the oil from her little bottle into the jars she acquired, until all the jars were filled with oil.

She didn't retaliate or say to Elisha, "I don't think you heard me right; I've only got a small bottle of oil, how could I fill all the jars that my sons collected from my neighbours?" Without hesitation, she did what Elisha (the man of God) told her to do and not just pay for her late husband's debt, but she also had some left-over money from the sales of the oil. She experienced God's supernatural miracle.

3. Another miracle Elisha did can be found in 2 Kings 4:8–37, where he made the Shunammite's woman son who died come back to life. And this happened in the Old Testament, before the Lord Jesus was born and walked on the earth He created. Elisha the prophet believed God and raised to life the son of the Shunammite woman. This woman, like Elisha, was a believer in God. She gave Elisha a place in the attic of her home to stay with her and her husband. Whenever Elisha and his servant, Gehazi, were in their region, she provided food and lodging for them.

This couple did not have children, and as a sign of gratefulness for what this woman and her husband did, Elisha prophesied to her that she would have a son. The following year his prophecy was fulfilled, she had a son. The boy grew up tagging along with his dad on the farm, a joy to his parents. But one day as he was with his dad, he became ill and died, so he called his wife who called to Elisha the man of God. And Elisha commanded his servant to place his stick in front of the boy's face to awaken the boy. But he wasn't awakened. So Elisha went to the boy's bed and **stretched himself out on the boy's body, praying to God**. The boy's body then became warm and the boy sneezed seven times and opened his eyes.

Elisha called out to his servant who called the mother of the child and presented him alive to his mum. She then fell at his feet, bowed to the ground, picked up her son, and went. She knew that Elisha was truly a man of God. The Supernatural power of God prevails when our human hearts touch God's heart.

4. I would like also to add the story of the king of Babylon who had a dream that disturbed his thoughts, and firmly decided that he wouldn't tell any of the wise men in his realm his dream, but he wanted them to interpret the dream that passed through his mind as he sat in his bed. And he added that if no wise men could tell him this dream, they would be killed. So **Daniel and his friends fasted and prayed to seek God's favour** (being Jews who believed in God and taken as captives in a foreign land) and reveal the dream and its meaning to him. **God then revealed to Daniel Nebuchadnezzar's dream and its interpretation.** As a result of this the king of Babylon lavished many gifts on him and made him ruler over the entire province. See Daniel chapter 2.

Due to the interpretation Daniel gave the king, he made an image of gold set up as a god. Nebuchadnezzar commanded that all people should now bow down to this image. But Daniel's three friends refused to bow down to King Nebuchadnezzar's image and were thrown into a burning furnace, set seven times hotter for these three men. **But they put their hope and lives in the hands of the living God who rescued them.** Nebuchadnezzar jumped to his feet seeing four men walking around in the fire unbound and unharmed, and **the fourth looked like God to him.**

And because of this experience, Nebuchadnezzar give a command that in his realm people should praise and exalt the God of Daniel and of these three brave men. All this recorded history can be found in the book of Daniel, chapters 2 & 3.

5. I too experienced a miracle of God without my immediate knowledge when **my two AA batteries in a small torch lasted for over two years, from March 1995 till about July 1997.** At the time I had just got divorced. I was living with my seven-year-old girl in a place where I couldn't even afford to hang proper curtains in my bedroom windows. It was also this time when I felt the Lord was drawing me closer to Him. During those years there wasn't a time where I wasn't contemplating God's goodness in my life. And I used to read my Bible every single night more than ever, armed with this torch with two AA batteries in it. All I remember was, after about two weeks reading my bible this way, the batteries got dimmer. And I remember saying to myself, "Oh no, do I need to buy a new battery now?" I turned my torch off and on, and then it became slightly brighter. So I used it over and over again without thinking about it, though sometimes switching it off and on again when it got dimmer, and it went back to normal brightness. This lasted until I remarried in April 1997.

Three months later David brought in a big jar of rechargeable batteries. And I remembered the two AA batteries in my torch and asked him, "How long would normal batteries last if you use it every night," showing him my torch. "Oh," he said, "I don't know, maybe about four weeks." With his response I clasped my hand over my mouth and said, "You know what I just experienced? A miracle without knowing it." I only had these two AA batteries in my torch since I bought it, when I moved in over two years previously. I had used this torch night after night without ever changing the batteries!

I don't believe I really had Supernatural faith in God in that experience. For I know I am as ordinary a Christian believer as any or most Christians are, but I feel the Lord gave this experience to me to dig even deeper into what I can know of Him. Because when that happened, I didn't even apply my faith, I just turned my torch off and on, but for sure I know it was my God's Supernatural goodness to me; for that's what I needed at that time. My worldly wealth was not sufficient, **so God extended the batteries' life to me supernaturally, to meet my needs** at that time. That's all I know. All the Praises and the Honour and the Glory all belong to HIM our God; for He truly is a SUPERNATURAL GOD.

And based on our relationship with the Lord Jesus and the Holy Spirit, He gives us Supernatural experiences. For instance, you've lost your ring and you know full well that you left it somewhere that you couldn't retrieve it, but there you found it in your jewellery case. Don't you feel so loved and valued by God when you experience His goodness, for He wants you to know you are loved and valued by Him? When we know God from our heart, not from our head, and we know that He fully loves us unconditionally, and when we have unity among our brothers and sisters in Christ, when we're together or even when were physically apart, but one in spirit with them, then whatever we ask of Him in prayer, we know we'll have it. Our petitions of Him don't have any hindrance; we'll receive from Him, according to the power that works within us, through His Son's Name, Amen.

2

DO NOT LIMIT GOD BY YOUR UNBELIEF

We cannot contain God in a small box of human imaginations. God is not subject to such a depleted human perception and we will never be able to contain or fully understand God's nature. We need to dig deeper in the nature of His unfailing love for us, not just our faith in Him. You know, **He made what's impossible for us in nature, possible for us in faith,** which we call miracles. Some Christians bind and limit God's power in their minds, but God is not subject to the limitations of our minds, or our imaginations; neither can we hold His power in our thoughts, or feelings. A lot of Christians confine God in the box of their limited natural imaginations, or thinking because they are so short of Godly experience due to unbelief. Their mind limits what God can do because of their lack of trust in God's power; they replace God's power with the nature of their experience. They think because something has never happened to anyone before, it will never happen now. Or have they forgotten what they read about people's faith in God? NOT because I experienced God's goodness in my life, about the two AA batteries, means I could boast about this as my faith. No, I can only inform you all that it was and always will be God's Supernatural goodness, because my LORD GOD knew what I needed at that time. When God steps into our situations, we begin to experience God's nature; which is **Supernatural to us**, but is **always 'the nature of God'**.

It says in Ephesians 3:20–21: *Now to Him* (the Lord

Jesus) *who is able to do (*all things*) exceedingly abundantly above all that we ask or think,* ***according to the power that works in us,*** (it's His power that works in us; it was He who gave us the power to do and to will. It only works in us when we are connected to the Source, our Supplier, the Lord Jesus and the Holy Spirit) *to Him be glory in the church and in Christ Jesus throughout all generations, for ever and ever! Amen.* **God honours our faith in action, when we honour His Word and His work.**

When no-one is checking and looking at you, in the secret place of your own home, is God at home in your heart? Who is God to you? Who is He in your thoughts? Are you scared to come close and tell Him all that is in your heart? How do you perceive Him in your imagination? What is your heart saying about Your God? Who is my Awesome and my Almighty God to you? Has He become big or little? What I mean is, who is God to you? Is He a big God or a little God to you? Is He the Boss in Your life? Do you show the Lord Jesus your appreciation, by telling Him "Lord, I come to You, because I know You love me. With sincerity of my heart I seek You, O God. I'm longing for Your Holy Presence, and I just want to be near You. I want to hear You again and again."? You know, when you feel thirsty for God's companionship and His presence, when you don't have peace in your heart and mind and you feel "He's so far away from me," **who stepped out of line, God or you?**

You know, when you just so want to have that essence of God's Sovereign joy and peace, and the joy of God's Holy Presence, when your soul is thirsty for the Living God, and you just want an embrace and fellowship with God and His Holy Spirit, what do you do? For me, whether I feel Him or not, I give thanks for the day, for His provision, for His faithfulness, that I still have my breath in me. I purposely remember all the good things He did in the past. I worship God, and examine my heart; His peace never leaves me. I read the bible, for God can speak to me through His words; whether I like it or not, what I do is always a decision. So decide that you are going to have a one-to-one with your loving God today. It's the evocative quality of God's love for us, and the sincerity of our love towards Him that brings us closer to God. His Holy Presence is what matters to me.

The reason I am writing this to you is so that you too may experience His goodness in your life. It's God's abundant grace He wants to perform in your life, so dare to believe God's Supernatural nature. I know a lot of Christians experience God miracles too, even now. God is not limited to a few, but is abundant to everyone who believes His unlimited power. It's inexhaustible.

But for some Christians today, they experienced His miracles because they believed in God's unlimited power: He is able to do all things for them according to His will. Or some might say, "It will never happen that way or this way." No, it won't—it will happen God's way, even when we are sometimes lacking in faith. God's love overcomes our unbelief so long as we remain in Him.

Another barrier in Christian believers for not experiencing God's healing or power is they have this hurry-up attitude; they don't want to wait for the presence of the Holy Spirit. When you're praying for someone and you see their impatient attitude in prayers, you get that feeling, *Do I have to carry on praying?* You feel that the person who is being prayed for is saying, "Hurry up, you" or even "Hurry up God, answer the prayers of this man or woman." Without actually saying it, it appears to me you're thinking, "Hurry up God, do what she or he says", or: "She's not really praying well, there's no change in me." Sometimes praying for believing relatives is harder because they know you. They normally have those pre-conceived thoughts of you and those 'hurry up, God, moments.' Sometimes it's easier to pray for a person who doesn't know you, and who is not a believer, but 'a hanger'. *I will hang on to see what will happen, if I wait.* And the reason I sometimes stay longer in prayer is I'm listening and waiting for the Holy Spirit to move in power so the person being prayed for gets impacted with what God is saying and doing then and there. **But if you're too impatient it is very disrespectful to God the Holy Spirit**, who moves in power on behalf of the person who is praying for you. Nevertheless, it says in 1 John 3:20–22: *If our hearts condemn us, we know that God is greater than our hearts, and He knows everything. Dear friends, if our hearts do not condemn us, we have confidence before God and receive from Him anything we ask, because we keep His commands and do what pleases Him.* This is for our own benefit knowing that what we ask for, we will receive, for our hearts do not feel condemned towards God, and we know God's favour rests on us.

You may ask, "What are the commandments?" It says in this passage in 1 John 3:23 & 24: *And this is His command: to believe in the name of His Son, Jesus Christ, and to love one another as He commanded us. The one who keeps God's commands lives in Him, and He in them. And this is how we know that He lives in us: We know it by the Spirit He gave us.* The commandment to love one another is to love God. For as you're loving others, you're showing your love and reverence to God, who gave us the commandments.

One time I couldn't pray properly because I felt so

unwell with flu. Maybe for over a week I would pray on and off, and I felt the Holy Spirit's presence was not as close to me as when I am well. He cannot dwell in an unclean place, and as we know, all sickness does not come from the Lord. Something bothered me, and I felt as if the Holy Spirit stepped aside; He couldn't touch me, as He's so Holy. It's almost like physically I was unclean, and I believe the Holy Spirit cannot come close to an unclean person (all illness is from the enemy, so when the enemy places something on you, even if only for a short time, you are physically unclean). God and the Holy Spirit are so holy that He can detect our uncleanness, so He could not come closer physically to touch me when I was unwell. The Holy Spirit did not leave me, I just felt slightly blocked or far away from Him. My sister who is a believer told me once that the Holy Spirit once left her, just to give her that experience, and she really felt unimaginably bad. She felt everything was ripped away from her. She was empty, and felt she had no hope, and was about to die. She could not explain everything she felt. That's why I know the Holy Spirit didn't leave me, He just maybe stepped aside, or maybe it was I who stepped away because my spirit He deposited in me can detect my own uncleanness. At that time of not feeling well, I messaged my daughter to pray for me. And the Lord revealed to me that **'the prayer of a mother the Lord always hears, but the prayer of a child goes straight to the throne of God.'** So teach your children to pray.

It says in Matthew 18:18: ***Assuredly, I say to you whatever you bind on earth*** (bind the spirit of sickness on earth) ***will be bound in heaven*** (then sickness will not be able to operate on earth as heaven declares, for in heaven GOD rules, above and over the earth) ***and whatever you loose on earth*** (God will loose the spirit of healing on earth) ***will be loosed in heaven*** (and it would be loosed in heaven, as the Lord Jesus declared). What a promise, what a statement. I see it as this: whatever God declares in heaven, the earth receives and puts it into existence, so whenever a righteous person (and only righteous due to the Lord Jesus' Righteousness—no one can boast) prays according to God's will, he will receive it directly from the hand of our Living Saviour!

I am not saying that Christians should never get sick or unwell. Since sin crept onto earth, we all experience some sort of illness; it's the nature on earth. But there are some illnesses that the Lord wants to release you from. Like it says in 1 Kings 15:23, **King Asa became diseased in his feet, but he did not seek God, only the physician.** So as far as I understand in this verse, there's some sort of illness when we need to seek God's healing; for He is the Greatest Physician. Seeking Him means humbling ourselves before God, saying (although not in literal words): "You have power above the knowledge of man and the medicine they prescribe." You are humbling yourself before God, knowing He knows best for you. That is why it says in Isaiah 53:5 … *by His wounds we are healed.* It means His body wounded for you. You have the entitlement of healing out of His sufferings. You will receive peace and healing when you believe!

I am not saying that all believers who don't get healed limit God and put Him in the box of their limited imaginations and have not enough faith. Who is a person that ever lived in this big bad world and saw all the goodness of God in their life, and was full to the brim all the time with faith in God? I have never seen or heard anyone yet. There's more to it than that.

I want to share the story of Jennifer Rees-Larcombe with you. (If you were a believer in the 1990s you would have probably heard her name and her story.) She became paralysed, and wheelchair bound for years and so many fascinating and interesting big well-known people in Christian circles prayed for her, but she didn't get healed.

In a conference she was attending, a new Christian believer felt in her heart to pray for Jennifer. And I believe for a baby Christian to offer a prayer to a person whom she only met at the conference, and sitting in a wheelchair, must have been a really daunting task. But this girl heard an instruction from the Lord and she wanted to obey God's voice. And because of Jennifer's experience of well-known preachers who prayed for her and she didn't get healed, she was reluctant for someone she didn't know, and had met only in this conference, to pray for her. Nevertheless, when other people in the conference persuaded her, she felt she would have nothing to lose if she was prayed for by this new Christian believer—a complete stranger. She reluctantly agreed for her to pray, and she got completely healed! Hallelujah! She went into the conference sitting in a wheelchair and went out of the conference walking. She herself put her wheelchair at the back of the car of her friend who brought her to the meeting. Praise God!

We cannot underestimate the power of God's presence at the right time and place, and the person whom God (the Lord Jesus) is going to choose for one's healing. So every opportunity we have should never be missed because of experiences we had in the past.

But for some people who have a gift of healing and cannot extend their own faith for themselves (I heard at least one, and I believe her), that barrier in their mind is not lack of faith, but sometimes we have our own limitations that only the Lord God could remove from our minds. They have faith for others to get healed and people they pray for completely get released from their sufferings. So when we hear of someone in this situation, we need to understand them where they are; and we need to pray for God's mercy and grace to envelop them, so they could be healed.

Probably that's when we need other brothers and sisters whom we have not met yet to pray for us, although we need to have discernment about who we are going to allow to touch us and pray. We definitely need the Holy Spirit's leading.

We know it's not always through the spiritual gift of a person who is famous for praying for the sick and they got healed that God always works. Sometimes with the knowledge and experience we see and hear, we remove our focus on **'The Ultimate Healer'**—the Lord God Himself.

Sometimes, when those Christians that have a gift of healing, hear, see, and experience **the healing touch of God** in someone's body, they may think they can just make healing happen by the knowledge they have of God's goodness. But maybe, and this is just maybe on my part saying this, that when we became so familiar with the gift of healing we are operating in, we think we are the one to pray for this and that person so that God could heal her or him. I think even though we have the gift of healing, we need to step back sometimes and let others pray, unless the Holy Spirit is really urging you to pray in certain situations. Of course, you wouldn't want the gift to be stagnant in you, but you need to let others have a chance to use the gift the Lord God is building in them.

As I said, God looks at the heart, not the face and His gift. If you are getting a bit obsessed to pray, step back and ask the Lord God, the Holy Spirit, "Lord, am I getting to want the glory for myself, and not give it to

You?" We probably think it's through us; may I not think like that, since a few people I prayed for, got healed. Oh, help me, God, not to be *healing* focused, but *Healer* focused. Amen.

All I know is this: it's God's will for us to experience His goodness, the reality of His love, and His Power over the work of the enemy in our lives. And He wants us to have that continual relationship with Him, without putting ourselves above other believers, our brothers and sisters in the Lord, immaterial of which continent we are living in.

3

THE POWER OF FORGIVENESS

Forgiveness first of all is a decision; it's like love! Love is a decision to stay with your husband and to stay with your wife for as long as both of you are alive, through good times and bad times. As it says in Ecclesiastes 7:14: ***When times are good, be happy; but when times are bad, consider this: God has made the one as well as the other***. So it means there's a way out, you wouldn't always be in the bad times, although it may look like that all the time.

God is the author of forgiveness and love. You might say, "But I hate that person." The power is in your decision, not based on feelings—because feelings are fickle and very changeable, but based on the situation. So you need to forgive, even if you don't feel like it.

Unforgiveness has the power to trap people in situations they cannot release themselves from, in the natural way of thinking. It's all in the mind, and goes deeper to the heart, and is damaging to the soul. A wave of thought came to mind, *I wonder if there is any unforgiveness in the animal kingdom?* Being serious now, unforgiveness has the power to take away your joy and your peace; sometimes it makes you feel ill, while forgiveness has power to take away your pain, and make you peaceful and joyful again. You might ask, "Where and how would I be able to take this pain and fear away? Well it's stated in Matthew 6:12–15: *And forgive us our debts, as we also have forgiven our debtors*. Verse 14:

For if you forgive other people when they sin against you, your heavenly Father will also forgive you. In verse 15 it says: *But if you do not forgive others their sins, your Father* (who is powerful God) *will not forgive your sins.*

You might say, "Why would I have to consult the Bible?" It is because you can use the Bible as your manual in life; it tells you about everything you need to know in life. When you don't know how to cook some dishes, you can look online at the BBC Good Food recipes, for example; so it's the same. When you don't know where you are going to leave your bad feelings or the pain and hurts you're carrying, you can go to the Bible and you will see the answer there. Then follow it step by step, the same as you would follow a recipe.

Unforgiveness hinders you from experiencing God's inexhaustible love and miracles. Sometimes people cannot receive complete healing due to unforgiveness in their hearts. God is a heart watcher. When your emotion is disturbed, the Holy Spirit cannot connect with you; it blocks the flow of God's presence in your own life, and you will feel the peace of God leave you, because He cannot enter your heart. That's why the word of God said we need to forgive. And we need each other, we cannot do it alone; we need other people's faith and gifting.

Jesus said, *"Love your neighbour as yourself."* As you love others, you're expressing your love not just to your neighbours but to God too. When we have unity, God commands a blessing for us, because unity with our brothers in the Lord honours Him.

Have you ever experienced that the minute you wake up in the morning you're already struggling with angry thoughts? You're not even thinking of anything else specifically when the person that pained you, without consciously thinking of them, entered your mind. And the minute it enters your mind, your hurts and anger rise again in you, and you're emotionally stirred up all over again. It's like you have no rest for it. That's the trick of the enemy; wherever you go and whatever you're doing it's present in your mind. Because the mind is the stronghold of the enemy, and the mind is connected to emotions. That's why it says in Romans 12:2: *And do not conform to this world, but be transformed by the renewing of your mind, that you may prove what is that good and acceptable and perfect will of God.*

When those hurtful experiences enter your mind, do not entertain them. Declare this to yourself: "Lord, I've forgiven them (when you've already done so), I am giving them again over to You; I lay them down again at the foot of Your Cross." And then ask the Holy Spirit to guard your heart and clear your mind of all the rubbish the enemy tried to remind you of and inflict on you.

Here's an example of casting out bad thoughts in you when it affects your focus. A friend of mine told me she was going to a Christian meeting once, to tell her testimony of how she became a Christian. She was really familiar with the place she was going to, when without apparent reason she realised she was on the wrong road, and she was lost. She recognised it was the enemy's device that made her lose her concentration as she was driving. So she stopped the car, wound the window down, and said, "Get out of my car, Satan, in the name of Jesus." Then she drove back and reached the place on time. She had to do something out of the ordinary and command the enemy to leave.

Heart, mind and soul are the three integral parts of your being that the enemy touches, and makes you slave to the thoughts inflicted on your mind, if you allow him.

Even if you don't, he impresses on you the painful past. I'm not saying you have invited him in, no. Without your conscious decision or thought he imposes on your mind, and barges into your memory to cripple your emotions and make you angry again. And when you feel angry, you also feel far away from God, and the Holy Spirit leaves. Why? Because it has disturbed His place in your heart when you have disturbed thoughts or emotions. The Holy Spirit cannot dwell there; it's like He can feel He's not welcome in your heart. You're entertaining the enemy, so He's got no place to sit on, in your heart, if you know what I mean?

What the enemy does is he just plonks or dumps in your head bad thoughts, so you will revisit, or recall, and be reminded of what you've done or you didn't do in the past, even if it's years ago or yesterday. The devil is always busy digging in and plugging in your memory all the bad experiences you've had. The devil would whisper memories to you that you never knew why you thought of them, and why they entered in your mind in the first place to make you busy with those thoughts again, no rest. He would want to hang around with you like a bad smell, so you start to carry bad thoughts for him all over again. Resist him by telling him who you are in God. Declare to yourself before God, "My Lord, my God, who loves me and died on the Cross for me, has carried all my infirmities for me. So I don't need to carry those things I don't need to carry; all you bad thoughts, you're not from the Lord Jesus; get away from me, in Jesus' Name."

The Lord Jesus gave us a remembrance of Himself in us. He left us the sign of His Covenant in the palm of our hands. Just look at the palm of your hands and you will see the sign of the Cross on them. The sign of the Cross signifies forgiveness—the Lord Jesus' forgiveness of our sins to reconcile us to God the Father, and He alone has the power of forgiveness.

Without the Lord Jesus' death and resurrection, there is no forgiveness; and without our cooperation with God, the Holy Spirit, we cannot just forgive. So if the Lord Jesus' solution for human sins is forgiveness, we too need to forgive those who harmed us, and release them that we may be able to release ourselves from them.

But if you don't want to release by forgiving the person who hurt you, you've imprisoned yourself with him, having the devil as the prison guard in your prison cell (your thoughts). And if you want to be healed from your illness or pain, you have to forgive others. By doing so, you're acknowledging that the Lord Jesus' sacrifice is an absolute exchange for the little or massive suffering you're experiencing right now.

This is the thing: once you forgive, you can ask the Lord Jesus to clear out your memory of them. It's like clearing out your cupboard of unusable stuff; those out-of-date things that would not be good for you, or might even become poison to your body if you use them. The devil is poison to you!

When you expect a rest for your weary soul, and you refuse to forgive, it's like grasping something by your hand, but your hand is already full of what someone has left you with to hold onto.

But if you surrender your mind and thoughts, even your heart and emotions (your own soul), your own past and present hurts to God, He will take care of them all for you. Because the Lord Jesus doesn't want you to be in pain all the time, He wants you to be set free from the grip of the enemy. That's why He carried all things for you, so you don't have to carry them all alone. Give them to the Lord, for the Lord Jesus gave them to God the Father. On the cross Jesus shouted, *"Forgive them*

Father, for they know not what they are doing," see Luke 23:34.

God will heal you and take care of you, if you let Him. God looks at the heart, and forgiving someone is a conscious decision to let them go, setting them all free (no baggage left for them to carry) and you get out of prison as well. You're not to be their judge, leave it to God.

The Lord Jesus Himself through the outworking of the Holy Spirit could help you let go of your pain (I know it's not always easy). The pain in the soul is real and sometimes so deep that you want revenge, and it's normal to feel that way as we're human beings. There's a tug within us not to let go, that's natural too, but that pain can destroy you.

I know you need to be real before God. Your pain is real; it's not imagined, it's not just a bruised ego, it needs to be dealt with in reality. And the honest thing you can do is to pour out your heart to God. God is aware of your pain and He doesn't want you to keep back from Him some of your pain and pretend to Him that you are okay. No, He really wants you to be gut level honest with Him, so that you can stop walking in pain. (He's probably whispering to you, "Give it to Me, give it to Me, My child.) He wants you to be free of pain. The Lord Jesus can extend His hand of grace to cover you, and erase your grief, your sorrow, and even your planning of revenge; yes, that too.

If you can be brave enough (with gut level honesty) to ask the Lord Jesus to overshadow you, and heal your emotions, and take the pain away from you, only then may you be able to truly forgive the person who put a scar in your heart, and put a hole in your soul. It may take time, but the Lord wouldn't rush your healing; He will be gentle with you, He will not force you to reject what you feel, but will enable you to face it with Him, not on your own, and not with your own strength.

Little by little you will be able to open your heart to the Lord Jesus. And when you do, put your heart in the hand of God. He will not crush it, but hold it gently, gazing at it over and over again, until your pain subsides. Wouldn't you want that for yourself?

So stop carrying revengeful thoughts in your heart (it's ever so heavy isn't it?). Instead, place it down gently in the merciful Hand of God. He will give you peace and comfort. The Lord Jesus will enable you to forget your pain and give you joy instead, and heal your memory until it doesn't hurt any more.

You know, when you mention someone's name and it still brings up pain in you, and tears flow down your checks and your eyes get misted, it means you are not completely healed yet. But when recounting painful events and your pain has subsided and it doesn't bring tears to your eyes any more, that's when you can really tell that you have forgiven. So that you may bless those who hurt you with the blessing the Lord God has for you both. It's like whatever you give to anyone, the same thing you will receive for yourself.

Don't worry about what you unlawfully received; cling instead to what God has for you. Peace is better than turmoil. Forgiveness is a command, not a concession. And when you have peace in your heart and soul, you feel satisfied and contented; who wouldn't want that in life?!

Opening your heart before God is the key to receiving God's forgiveness. God wants you to empty your heart of pain and offence to Him, so that God can fill your heart with His love and joy—for yourself first, that is the key. You cannot love others if you don't know how to love yourself. You need to experience the true love that comes from God. Only after you receive God's love and forgiveness for yourself will you be able to forgive and love others. That why it says in James 4:2b *You have not, because you ask not.* **So it means you cannot give what you haven't got**. If you didn't ask God to forgive you, you cannot extend that forgiveness to others, because you didn't have it in you to give it away in the first place. But if you ask God for His forgiveness, you will receive His forgiveness. He can identify with you, because He extended His forgiveness to those who nailed Him to the Cross and then He offered forgiveness to us.

If you say, "Why does it have to be me first who asks for God's forgiveness?" It's because it's you who recognised you're carrying unnecessary pains of unforgiveness in your heart. **The Human heart is God's window for checking the temperature of your soul.**

If you won't forgive, you will end up feeling bitter, and you will only continually hurt yourself. Bitterness is a thief; it steals your joy, your peace, and it saps away your strength, and in the end it will make a person ill. Even the doctors know this is a well-known truth.

Unforgiveness is a sin and the biggest hindrance for healing. Forgiving someone who wronged and hurt you is a must concerning healing and spiritual growth. Immediately after the Lord Jesus taught His disciples how to pray (we know the prayer, Our Father, who art in heaven…), this is what the Lord told them: Matthew 6:14–15: *For if you forgive other people when they sin against you, Your heavenly Father will also forgive you. But if you do not forgive others their sins, your Father will not forgive your sins also.* (Who is a person alive today and never sins?) And it says in James 5:16: *Therefore: confess your sins to each other and pray for each other so that you may be healed.* (There's healing after forgiveness, fact!) The prayer of a righteous person is powerful and effective, but when a husband does not treat his wife rightly, his prayers are hindered, see 2 Peter 3:7. **Our prayers become effective when God is enthroned in our hearts**. We become righteous due to the Lord Jesus' righteousness, not our own. We do not have an ounce of it, until the Lord Jesus extends His righteousness and covers us with His own righteousness. When we remain in His Words and teaching, not reasoning out, or fighting with human explanation, then we close the door to the enemy. Then the Lord will release that person from your memory, and release your emotional agony out of him or her. The more you remember the sin they've done to you, the more you prolong your pain.

The Lord God is a heart watcher, and He responds to a heart that is not hard but pliable in His hand.

It says in Mark 11:25: *"And whenever you stand praying, if you have anything against anyone, forgive him, that your Father in heaven may also forgive you your trespasses."*

And you know why unforgiveness is so heavy to carry, because you have no rest for it and you can never put it down; it's with you wherever you go. When you wake up in the morning it's there, when you go to bed at night, it's there in your head, when you're alone, it niggles in your thoughts. It makes you angry, you cannot get rid of it in your head and in your emotions, and there's no rest for your weary soul (it really dictates the state of your heart's condition day by day), not even for a very short time. It's like carrying a 20-kilogram sack of potatoes that you cannot put down to have a rest. Unforgiveness is always present wherever you are, that's why it makes you weary. Even in the company of friendly and good people who love you and care about you, you will still feel restless; it wearies your soul, and you cannot forget it or put it in a drawer.

When the feeling of wanting revenge on the person who harmed you comes to mind again, especially when you have already forgiven them, shut out the thoughts in your head. Once you recognise it, resist it. Ask the Holy Spirit to help you stop taking back the memory of your pain. So that every time that person who hurt you pops into your mind, make it a conscious decision to invalidate your feelings there and then, by saying to the Lord Jesus, "Lord, I have forgiven them." Keep on asking the Holy Spirit to guard your heart and mind. This is the advantage of being a born-again Christian; you can say a quick prayer like this: "Lord Jesus, cover me with Your precious blood, from the top of my head to the soles of my feet; so the enemy will see Your red blood in me and flee away from me, in Jesus' Mighty name I pray, Amen.

When you withhold unforgiveness it's like a double whammy for you. Because you are already hurt by them, and you will be continuously hurting yourself by carrying the memory of your pain in mind, it's exhausting. You need to be conscious of your decisions. Whatever you wish for someone, good or bad, sometimes you reap what you sow.

Even when you're thinking that God loves me, and that He is on my side, do not try to get your own back. God's love is not one sided, He loves both you and the person or persons who hurt you, equally. He cannot help loving all humanity, that is God's nature, LOVE.

Real forgiveness comes from the heart. But the mind is the integral part the enemy attacks us on, and this is the same sense we can use against the enemy to win a battle over him. It's all in the mind! We have to guard our minds, for whatever touches our mind touches our heart, and when our thoughts and emotions are affected, we make negative decisions. But when we use the WORD of God, and declare the Lord Jesus' victory on the Cross, our focus shifts to His power over our circumstances and we win the battle. We have to remember to stand on God's Word and submit ourselves under the fellowship of the Holy Spirit, then we will always be on the winning side.

This is the benefit of having the Lord Jesus as your Saviour: you can unload onto Him the heavy burden of your soul.

How to forgive and how to receive forgiveness

We have to remember that the person who hurt you is the tool the devil uses against you. We know the enemy doesn't have permission to tickle your brain with all his nonsense.

First step: Get alone with God.

Matthew 6:6: *But you, when you pray, go into your room, and when you have shut your door, pray to your Father who is in the secret place; and your Father who sees in secret will reward you openly.*

Go to your room, close the door, turn your phone off, and any computer games or anything that may disrupt you. Sit up on your bed and close your eyes so you can focus on yourself and on God.

Second step: Start praying.

If you're saying to yourself, "I don't how to pray," let me tell you, praying is just talking, it's like gossiping. Now start gossiping to God; tell Him who the person is who hurt you and explain how it happened. If you feel that you're partly in the wrong, then admit your mistake between you and God. But if you feel all the wrongdoing is from the other person, this is your chance to tell the Lord Jesus everything you must be feeling, oozing out your whole emotions, your pain, and even regrets. Mention all what you're feeling, even admitting "Lord, I'm angry", or "I really hate this person" or "I feel betrayed." If you need to stay longer just crying out to God all your pain, don't hold back—just do it. Say, "Lord, I give You my pain. (**By going through this you are releasing your pain to God**—it's like cleansing your soul.) Then say this, "Lord Jesus, help me to forgive … (mention their names and what they did to you). Then ask the Lord Jesus to help to remove from your heart all the feelings of anger, bitterness, resentment, fear and betrayal etc.

Continue to ask the Lord Jesus to help you forgive, from your heart, and to erase all the memory and scarring that he/she caused you, and to cleanse you by His own blood. By going through this step it's like casting out all your anxieties, pain and anger on Him, who cares for you.

Third step: Ask the Lord Jesus to help you forgive yourself and to receive His peace, to overshadow you by His Holy Spirit and make you whole. As you feel released from all that unnecessary carrying of emotions, give God the glory and praise due to Him.

So this is how you forgive and receive God's forgiveness for yourself.

If you're not a believer yet, just try these steps and see what the Lord Jesus can do for you. He knows what it was like to be treated so unfairly—spat on, nailed on the Cross hands and feet, and ultimately died for your sins and mine.

Forgiveness means taking away the pain and anger off you … and giving it to God, who has the power over your pain, and will release you from it.

It says in 1 Peter 5:7: *Casting all your care upon Him, for He cares for you.* Casting means you letting it go. And casting is the opposite of keeping. When you are holding on to the anger and pain it means you are keeping it for yourself. It's like you're taking care of it, you don't want to put it down or let go, you're guarding it. So you always have the responsibility of maintaining it.

But when you cast it, it means you let go of it, and who is better to hold it than the One who has been through it already and won? And since He knows you better than you know yourself, He actually wants you to be set free from the tormenting attack in your heart and head that is straining you and makes you feel helpless. But help is offered to you when you give it to God in prayer. There's a song that goes: *O what peace we often forfeit, O what needless pain we bear, all because we do not carry everything to God in prayer.*

4

SHE CHALLENGED GOD, AND GOD RESCUED HER

My mum was an orphan when she was five years old, so she was passed on to relatives and lived with them. When she was a bit older, she had no choice but to help them with everyday chores. (It was an unsaid repayment of gratitude.) She had never been a child for long as she had to grow up so quickly, as quickly as the days and weeks and months passed by. It's obvious that she never had a good childhood experience and had no proper education at all. (She could only write her name because my older brother and sister taught her, but she forgot how to write her own name when she became older, my poor mummy.)

I remember her telling me that her aunt would send her to school for two days or up to two weeks, and then she had to stay home again to help her aunt for months and months. When someone from the school asked her aunt why my mum (Noria Tirol, that's her name) was not attending school, she would send her to school for a day or two and then keep her at home again to help her. This carried on again and again until in the end no-one ever came to ask about her education.

Mum didn't elaborate on what kind of work she did, but I could imagine it included washing the clothes by hand, cleaning the house, making every step in her aunt's house shiny and cooking for her aunt's family. This aunt of hers was sometimes unkind, and slightly mean and horrible to her. She accused mum of stealing something when she knew mum couldn't hide anything from them; she was living with them and she was only a child. One particular time she remembered most was when her aunt accused Mum of eating an egg she did not have, simply because she had hiccups. You know, it was just an egg, but at that time Mum was punished because she refused to tell a lie, or be interrogated by her aunt. Mum told her she was not lying; she never had that egg. Because Mum stood up for herself and answered back, **she was beaten so badly that she felt such bitterness in her soul. She was bruised and in so much pain and agony that she could hardly walk**. *The day is coming when I will leave the whole lot of you*, she promised herself. It's obvious that it was not the only time she had been beaten up.

"You know," she told us, "I had no-one to turn to, and everyone seemed against me, though I didn't do anything wrong or do what they were accusing me of. **I felt like heaven and earth collided in me and crushed me inside; and nobody cared if I lived or died.** If only my parents were still alive, they could have helped me," she wished. Alone and with no-one to confide in, **in the bitterness of her soul she said to herself, "Oh I wish there was God in heaven looking down at me, and fighting my case."** When she was telling us her story, I felt really sad for my mum, but she was just reminiscing; she wasn't angry or crying any more.

So she decided to leave her aunt's house and was determined to escape and go to her other aunt. Though she lived far away from them, this aunt was a bit kinder to her than the one she was staying with, whenever she had visited them.

She was in such a state of mind and distressed that the only way Mum knew she could reach her other aunt quicker was to pass by this place which was part forest part cave. My mum told us that people around them expressed that there were some sorts of demonic forces in that area, where no-one ever tempted to pass by after midday. It was dark but not just lacking daylight, rather darkness that you can feel; it was spiritually evil. Those who knew the place told her they could sense and hear eerie sounds and see frightening visions.

A few people who tried to brave it and ventured out there said they kept on walking, and their own mind confused them. They never reached where they we're heading for, and they arrived back again at the place where they had started, although they had walked for the whole day. And when you're there they said that you'll be hearing and seeing thing that are difficult to describe. So that's what Mum heard about this place. She never entered that forest as she was frightened after hearing that people around them said that a demonic presence exists there.

But my mum was in inconsolable pain, exhausted and truly hurt; not just physically, but mentally and emotionally. She felt pain within her soul and she said she had had enough! (She knew in her heart she didn't do anything wrong; her aunt's accusations were not true.) She desperately wanted to escape to go to her other aunt's home, who lived miles away from them. And the only route she knew where they would not follow her (especially at night) was to enter through this demonic place where everybody else dared not tread after midday.

It is true that desperate people do desperate actions; they would even hold a sharp knife by the blade (though you know it will cut you) if that's the only way out. And that's where my mum was at that particular time in her life.

On my mum's way to her other aunt, she told me (well I mean, she told all of us, including my brothers and sisters) that **she challenged God** and said, "OH

GOD … LORD GOD ALMIGHTY … IF IT IS TRUE THAT THERE IS GOD IN THIS WORLD; SAVE ME, HELP ME, GUIDE ME." The minute those words came out of her mouth (guess what?), **she saw the Lord Jesus turn up by her side. He opened His Arms wide, covered her, as if He had wings, protected her and the darkness around them became light (this part reminded me of *God is light and in Him there is no darkness at all*, see 1 John 1:5)** and all the scary sounds of birds and frightening human sounds were lifted off, everything was lighted and the place became quiet. The Lord Jesus just walked with Mum; they didn't have any conversation. On her way to her other aunt she felt at peace and she wasn't scared any longer. When she was near her other aunt's home, (it's obvious the Lord guided her way to her aunt) the Lord Jesus stood a bit further away and waited for her to reach the other side of the clearing, and He illuminated her way to her aunt's house.

When the door was opened to her, her aunt said, "All night long, this all night long we couldn't go to sleep; we felt we were waiting for someone to come. We just could not go to sleep at all, and it's you." (She arrived at her aunt's home at two o'clock in the morning.) Mum told them everything that had happened, including being guided and protected by the (Angel she told them) Lord Jesus, and that they walked through this forbidden place. The minute the Lord walked in that place, everything was illuminated and went quiet; wherever they turned there was bright light everywhere.

My mum, who was 4 feet 8 and a half inches tall, told us that she challenged God. But I don't believe that was a challenge to God, I reckon she called on God (that's what she did), for this is what it says in Jeremiah 33:3: ***Call to Me, and I will answer you, and show you great and mighty things, which you do not know.*** Also in

Jeremiah 29:13 & 14 it says: ***And you will seek Me and find Me, when you search for Me with all your heart. I*** (**God**) ***will be found by you*** ....

And in Psalm 34:6 it says: *This poor man called, and the Lord heard him; he saved him out of all his troubles.* My mum never knew how to read the Bible, but the practical application of God's word in her life she experienced in times of her need.

And I believe, before even mum opened her mouth in challenging God as she says, God was already looking at her heart and knew what she was about to say to God. And I'm so grateful that God looks at the heart and knew my mum's heart. I praise God for His goodness to my mum, and I'm glad she shared her story with us; she really put her hope in God.

People in the Philippines, especially in Mum's era, go to bed the minute it gets dark, which is maybe half past five or six o'clock in the evening and wake up at about four o'clock in the morning. Her aunt told her it was only on that particular evening when Mum was on her way to them (her aunt's home) that they all felt they couldn't go to sleep, waiting for someone to come; they didn't know who was the person coming until Mum turned up and knocked on their door. Now I know and realise there wouldn't be any electric lights in the remote places of the Philippines, even now. I didn't even know such a place existed in those days, as mum described the forest; but that was her era.

After a few more years had passed, an arranged marriage for my mum was made by her aunt and uncle to a man who became a soldier during the second-world war. Her husband wasn't a very good man. Mum lived with all his family, but after they had two children, my mum decided to escape again, this time (for good) away from her husband and his family.

Fortunately, my mum remembered her late dad's friend who owned ships that travelled outside Visayan Island, where my mum came from. Her first born girl (my eldest sister) and Mum came on board and landed in Bauan, a sea port in Batangas. Her second child, a son, died during the war; she was devastated. It was the last straw for her, that's why she decided to leave, so just the two of them, Mum and her girl. My granddad's friend, although old (not as old as my grandad, I expect), helped mum to escape her hard life. He even helped her to gather her few possessions, which was just clothing and a daughter. This man was very kind to Mum and my sister; I Thank God for him.

After landing in Bauan, Batangas, she found a job, working in the kitchen of a small cafe, but after about eight months working there, she fell ill. The conditions were atrocious; her clothes would get wet and then dry on her body through her perspiring all the time. She had contracted pneumonia. Her employer gave her a few days off to get better. They found her a quack doctor, who in the end became her mother-in-law. Yes, my grandmother on my father's side was a quack doctor. I remember seeing her write some letters on a little piece of paper, put plant sap on it, stick it on people's forehead, leave it for three days, not wetting it, and eventually they felt better.

My grandfather's name on my mum's side of the family was Rafael Helito-Tirol. He was a land owner and owned a lot of land. Year after year they harvested copra, sugar cane, coffee, and other products—whatever seemed to be growing on their land. My grandad was quite a wealthy man in his time. He used to speak to his dogs and command them in Spanish. It's obvious he was an old Spanish man. Mum told us how he died: He was walking along his property one day, when a coconut fell from a tree and hit him on the head; it cracked his skull and he died.

She remembered that her aunt said he was about eighty years old when he died. (I'm not sure if it was his real age.) After his death, his land was divided up by his family, so her aunts and uncles now owned their land. And my Grandma (Mum's mum), named Irenea Santo-Tirol, was probably his third wife. Mum was the middle daughter of three. Both her sisters died of the same illness. Her eldest sister died when she was a teenager, but she didn't grow up with them so she didn't really know much about them. My Gramps (that's grandma and grandpa) separated before Grandad died, but grandma had her fourth child that my mum never saw when she was in Visayan Island although she had heard of her.

But Mum saw her youngest sister and her children when we were a lot older. They came and stayed with us, together with her granddaughter for a week. So we met them too, but I wouldn't remember them that much, apart from her granddaughter pulling my only necklace off my neck, breaking it and then lying about in front of her grandma. She told her that I gave her the necklace. I couldn't say a word.

They didn't keep in touch, and we too didn't communicate with them. Some of them lived in Manila; we met them once and that's it. But Mum went back home to Visayan island after over forty years living in Batangas. She met a few or her living relatives.

I asked Mum once when her birthday is, but she didn't really know when she was born. That's when she mentioned that her aunt said that the hair of the corn was popping out of its husk at the time she was born. Because mum knew all our birthdays, and we sometimes celebrated them when we had the money, Mum must probably have felt left out, not knowing when she was born. So she told me that she prayed and asked the Lord once, **"Lord, when was I born, when is my birthday?" And the Lord answered and told her, "September 18th 1920, Saturday."**

When the Lord gave her an answer it was complete; the date, the year, even the day she was born. Okay, there's no actual time, but I believe time only applies on earth, time doesn't exist in heaven, who knows! The Lord moves in His own time, no limit. (My mum's name must be written in the book of life!) So we celebrated her birthday whenever we could, every 18th of September each year. Perhaps sometimes we need to ask the Lord questions that we do not know, not in a disrespectful sense, but in those wondering moments, when we do not have a clue.

Unfortunately, my mum passed away on the 1st of December 2018 at the age of 98. For me, that was a life well lived. My mum's story concerning the goodness of God in her life is not buried with her, it's alive here in the pages of my book, where she was grateful how the Lord moved His hand on her behalf and rescued her. I am sharing here with you all the goodness of the Living God who answers the call from the heart, in the story of my mum, who said she "challenged God" and "God rescued" her!

How could we crown You, O God, except with the Testimony of Your goodness to us—the prayers You answered—and all the good things we experience through Your fascinating love! I Praise You and Thank YOU, O Lord God Almighty!

One of the ladies who heard of my story told me, "Your mum had a big influence on your faith. I was brought up as a Catholic too," she said, "but I never heard anything about Godly experiences like your mum had, from my own mother." I told her that perhaps I would write my mum's story—her personal experiences. And so here I did.

One particular lady (a colleague) said that I have deeper faith than she could imagine, and was amazed at where I got this deeper faith in God from. She was sort of wondering, almost asking, but not really saying, if you know what I mean. I was thinking, "Yeah, where did I get this belief in God?" I was thinking to myself then that it was personal experience; now I realise, well … if you have a mum who challenged God, and proved that God is real and truly exists, and had experiences of HIM, and God helped her when she was desperately asking for help ... well I suppose because of what I heard from my mum, I believed. Wouldn't you believe the stories your own mum told you? I was especially fascinated when she told me about her dream that she reached heaven.

Hearing Mum's story I became more fascinated with her, and desperately wanted to have the same dream as hers so I prayed, "Lord I wish, I wish I could see heaven just like Mum." I prayed over and over again for a few nights. And then one night I had a dream. In my dream I was alone, standing in an unfamiliar place .... All of a sudden a man appeared next to me. "Who is this man?" I said to myself, "And what is he doing here?" He had long hair and wore a long white robe.

He extended his hand and said to me, "Come."

"Hold on," I thought, "he is a stranger .... Where is he going to take me? My mum warned me not to go with strangers."

Nevertheless I reached out to him. I was about to step forward when something caught my attention; a narrow road, gloomy and dusty with a little flickering street light. There were quite a lot of people coming and going. I pointed this to the man who was with me but he said,

"NO, this is the way!"

He was leading me along to this very tiny criss-cross like wire, not even a path. I could only see it when my foot touched it. I thought it might hurt my feet, but it didn't so I continued walking with him. It was dark and there was no proper path in this place. The criss-cross wire only appeared when my little feet were on it. I could see rubble, thorns and bushes all around my feet.

At the end of my walk, right in front of me was a huge mountain. I asked the man if I had to climb up but he had disappeared. I looked back to find any route, but there was nothing; no path, no other visible way I could go to. I was standing for a while trying to find out how I could go back but there was no other way; I was worried I couldn't go home, I just had to climb this enormous mountain.

I looked from side to side to see what was beyond this mountain but I could not see a thing. This mountain was very high and extremely wide. What could I do? "I will be stuck here forever if I don't do anything," I mumbled to myself. So I decided I had to climb this mountain; I wouldn't be able to leave this place if I just stood here. There was no escape now, I had to do it.

It was such a struggle to reach the top. When I did, I came to a graveyard with a garden. I heard a voice call out, "Visitor!" But I didn't see anyone, and the voice seemed different, it didn't sound spoken! Then I saw a few ladies tending the garden. I looked around and the first thing that dawned on me was the calmness and peacefulness of this place. It was beautiful and serene and sunny, although the sun was not shining. I thought to myself, "This must be heaven."

I looked about in the garden to pick some flowers, but I heard a voice say, "NO!" I turned to see who was talking to me, no-one was near and everyone's back was turned. I carried on reaching for a flower, but a voice forbade me a second time, "NO!" I turned around again but the ladies were exactly in the same place the first time I saw them; they continued what they were doing as before. Fascinated with how beautiful the flowers looked, I carried on reaching for one; I was very persistent. For the third time I heard the voice say, "NO!" Again I turned around to see who was speaking to me but they were still far away from me.

By then I realised they knew my thoughts! Their thoughts were voices to me …. "Oh no," I gasped! They knew what I was thinking and I became aware of it. By this time one of the ladies came over. She was just standing next to me; we didn't exchange words or speak yet we understood each other. It was like that her thoughts were speech to me and vice versa. I heard another voice call out, "Visiting time is over," but I said to a lady who was with me, "Please don't let me go, I don't want to go anywhere, I like it here, this is my home." She didn't say anything, she walked along and I followed her. The next thing I knew I was at a graveyard for little children.

The lady who was looking after this place pointed out a tiny grave to me and said, "This is your brother's."

I thought, "A baby... as far as I know I am the youngest, who is this baby? I am sure there is no baby after me." I didn't realise she knew what I was thinking until she said, "Your mum told you all about him." I looked at the grave and I thought hard, "Oh yes, I remember," I replied, "my half-brother from her first husband; he died of the sort of illness that was prevalent during World War II." I paused and continued, "Mum told us she was absolutely devastated when this baby died, she loved him so much that she would not be able to forget him. He was such a lovely boy." I told her the story that my mum told me, with a sigh. Then she pointed at the lines of candles nearby.

"Do you see that," pointing at the shortest candle, "that is yours … **it is not your time yet**."

"Why is my candle the shortest one of all?" I asked. And it was burning rapidly I thought; so I stared at it for a while to see what would happen. Eventually it burned more slowly, and in the end the candle appeared to be the same length as when I first saw it.

"These candles belong to newborn babies," she replied.

I was about eight or nine at that time. Then I woke up …. "Mum! I reached heaven too," I squealed at her when I woke up. "And the lady in the graveyard showed me the grave of my brother." (He died when he was a baby.)

I told Mum the whole story of my dreams. "Everything seemed so real. I remember the time when you told us about your baby that died during the war. I only saw the grave, I didn't see his face," I confessed with sadness.

This made me believe in heaven when I was little. Even now I still believe that, for the real story of my little brother's was known there. I believed this was not just an ordinary dream and I promised myself I would be back someday to stay there forever, not as a visitor.

As a child who knew nothing apart from the true stories my mum told me, I suppose that's when I actually knew that there is God, and it became like an everyday part of life. (Faith is a deep word but I say believe—I truly believed in God.) Anyone who has a Godly encounter (including my mum) holds on to the experience and doesn't wish to let go of it. I am one of them, for I know God's goodness not just in my mum's life, but in mine too. God's love never expires; and now it renews my expectation of God. I thank You, LORD

GOD, for Your goodness to us.

When God answers your very own prayers, you could not say it's only a coincidence, when you actually asked God to help you. God's love for us is beautiful, peaceful, it's satisfying, it's liberating. This is God's love for those who believe in Him. When you know you are loved by someone and that someone is God, you have the confidence that He will respond to you when you call on Him, and make you joyful. And it's free access—you only need to be yourself to call on God.

I was only a child when I experienced that God answered my prayers. I once lost a ring in the sea and found it after I prayed a few times. Another time our family dog had been missing for three days, and I heard my dad say, "It will be dead by now." I cried and prayed and after another four days it came back; he saw me, came forward limping, looked me in the eye and curled up back where he was. Then I heard the Lord say, "That is his second life." So it means God brought my dog back to life because I prayed. A child's prayer is so effective.

Once, I wasn't well and asked my daughter to pray for me. I don't know if she did but this is the impression from my heart I heard from God: **"The prayer of the mother the Lord always hears, but the prayer of the child goes straight to the throne of God."** I suppose Mum was still a child when she had those experiences (she prayed from the innermost part of her being—her heart), when her prayers went straight to the throne of God and He rescued her. So teach your children to pray.

My mum told me another story when God answered her prayers. On her way to the market she prayed that she would find some money to buy us some food, for she didn't have enough fish or prawns to sell. As she walked and prayed she found a dirty handkerchief with a small amount of coins knotted inside it (it was a green and white handkerchief she showed me); it was enough to buy us food for that day.

This is the truth: the more you pray, the more God answers your prayers; your experience enables you to build a connection with Him, as He builds relationship with you, as His sons and daughters. **God is literally a Good, Good Father to all. I'm immensely appreciative of God's love and care, it gives me so much hope to be in Him.**

5

CATY'S TESTIMONY

It was quite a challenging time for Caty. Though she didn't say she challenged God, her actual attitude seemed to test or question God's availability or ability to respond to her.

Caty was born into a loving Christian family, one where her Dad was her best friend; they did everything together. When she was eight, disaster struck and he became ill. He was very absent and she didn't see much of him after that, and if she did, he wasn't nice any more. She used to cry to God that she had lost her best friend. She was emotionally wounded, abused and partially neglected during the rest of her childhood. She knew she was supposed to pray and God was supposed to fix things, but what do you do when He doesn't? Not knowing that God could actually talk back to her, she got angry at Him. She hated God for taking her best friend and leaving her a monster. She never doubted God existed but the only thing Caty felt towards this Creator was hatred.

In her teenage years, Caty was living her life away from God. Partier, Ice Queen as her friends used to call her. In fact, she prided herself back then on being the Ice Queen and being stone cold. When she used to come home from Uni, the only time she would get to spend with her mum would be at church as her mum had to work all the hours she could to support her Dad. The youth pastor of this church one day asked Caty if she would attend a youth camp they were organising; it was to host Christian young people from all over the world. Of course, she said no. There'd be no alcohol there, none of her friends and of course, they'd talk about God. But this pastor was very persistent and one day she told her she had promised these people from other countries a tour of London, and nobody knew London like Caty did, so would she please come. She agreed on the premise that she would not bow down and pray, worship, or even acknowledge her God existed. The youth pastor agreed with a big smile on her face. Caty was confused at her happiness but clarified she would have nothing to do with God.

Fast forward to this youth camp, Caty was not enjoying daily big group worship. She liked the food, the fun, the games … but she did not enjoy worship or learning about God.

In one of these big group sessions, she was tucked away in the corner of the room wary of all these people who were crazily prancing around and enjoying themselves, all the while singing to God. She wanted to be anywhere but there. She remembers closing her eyes wishing she could be back at uni on a night out with her friends, and as she sat there **she felt someone hug her**.

She opened her eyes shocked, thinking, *Why are you touching me? I love being cuddled, but I wish this person would ask my permission first.* (She said she gave off repelling vibes towards people in general.) She looked around, but no one was there. Maybe she had just imagined it. **She closed her eyes again, and someone hugged her a second time**. She opened her eyes, swung round and saw a brick wall. There was no one close to her. This time she did not close her eyes again. She thought she was going as crazy as all of the other people in the room and she didn't like it. As she sat there, scared, confused, wanting to hide, the most extraordinary thing happened. **She was hugged for a third time, in such a real and tangible way**. She looked down and **there were no visible arms around her, but this hug was so tight and comforting**. At this moment she felt something in her heart. She felt something change, and the Ice Queen who had never cried burst into tears there and then in the room. She felt truly loved for the first time in her life since she was a very small child. She remembers the youth pastor come running over and Caty just kept asking her, "Is it possible that God can really love me? Me?". It is possible, and true. The ultimate truth of her life is that she has always belonged, been loved and accepted.

Caty went to SOM heart school after it being prophesied over her that God would send her and provide the finances. During this time she had a lot of healing about her childhood and came to terms with a lot of the trauma she had experienced. Upon her return, things were still not easy but she had learnt that God doesn't always answer prayers in the way we expect. She told me He could have been wanting to reveal Himself to her as a Dad and show her unconditional love in ways her own father could not during that time. What she realised after all of this is that **God is a God of restoration**, because the circumstances around her Dad's illness haven't changed but her heart towards Him has. Since moving out of home, she has a great relationship with her Dad now—one she did not know that she wanted or needed. She says, "He is the one I go to when things are tough and I just need a hug. He is the one whom I share a lot of laughter with. **Forgiveness was key to unlocking this restoration—forgiveness and allowing God the room to change our lives** and relationship for the better. I have my Dad back and I am so grateful to God for him and the amazing things He has done for us."

I feel the Lord pursued Caty with His great love and tenderness where she was—in pain—and I believe that the cuddles the Lord gave her truly soothed away the sting of her pain from childhood. It was like she challenged God without words from her lips, but with a statement from her heart. For God looks at the heart, see 1 Samuel 16:7. And God never crushes a contrite spirit, but heals and soothes them who come to Him. The Lord managed to pull down the barrier off her, and gave her the experience (I could imagine such a gentle cuddle, no cuddle like she had experienced before) of His unchanging and unconditional love. I could only presume that her Godly experience put an indelible acknowledgement of God into the bottom of her heart. God's cuddles made her return to God, and she started a personal relationship with Him.

Growing up in a Christian home doesn't automatically mean one has a personal relationship with God. Everyone needs a personal revelation from the Lord God, no matter how deep your parents' or grandparents' relationship with God is. You cannot inherit it you must start your own personal walk with God for yourself.

6

HEALING

This is now a bit of my testimony. This year, in July 2020, at work I saw this lady sweating. Her face showed she was in such pain. She had crutches under both her arms, and she could hardly use both her arms freely. As I saw her struggling in this condition, I asked the Lord, "Do You want me to say something to this lady?" I heard the word "Pray." I don't know if it was my head or not, but I asked again, "Lord how about if she doesn't want me to pray?" I felt the Lord say, **"Ask, because if you don't pray, she wouldn't get healed."** Sometimes I do have a conversation with the Lord as I am working.

So when it was her turn for me to serve her, I said, "What happened to you?"

"Oh," she said, "I had a fall and twisted my ankle and broke my bones."

"Oh, that must be painful. How long ago did it happen?"

"Three months ago," and she continued, "and with this coronavirus the doctor would not be able to operate until two months or so."

"Are you in pain now?" I asked.

"Yes" she said.

So I found an opportunity to ask her, "Do you want me to pray for you; do you believe?"

"Oh yes, yes," she replied "I am a healer myself; I do Reiki healing."

I said, "Oh, it's different for me—I don't heal, I believe in God as a healer." And because I heard the

Holy Spirit tell me that "She wouldn't get healed if you don't pray," I asked her, "What is your name?"

She said, "Dawn," and I prayed for her. After I prayed, I asked, "Did you feel anything (I meant while I was praying)?"

"My bones are creaking on my ankle," she answered. She said thank you, paid for her shopping and then off she went.

The following Friday, the 24th of July, I saw her again but I didn't realise it was her. I asked, "How are you?" as I do sometimes with the customers.

She said, "Oh I can drive now."

I looked at her, and thought to myself, "Why is she saying to me she can drive now? I then realised, and responded to her, "Oh yeah, I prayed for you, I remember. But I can't remember if it was three days ago or a week ago.

"Yes" she replied, "thank you."

I asked her, "How long weren't you able to drive?" I can't remember if she said, two months or three months. I was so excited knowing God touched her ankle, recollecting her situation a few days back when she looked quite dreadful, but now she was trying to tell me she is now healed? Well, she's definitely not struggling, though I saw her move one crutch into her trolley. It's definitely not under her arm, so she's not using it. She looked a lot happier and thanked me again. We finished our conversation in such a short time and off she went. I haven't seen her again for a while now, but she's the first lady that came back to me this year (2020) to thank me for my prayers, and to show that she's been healed.

In her case I can really see the goodness of God, and how humble God is, and so, so good to all, even though this lady did not fully believe in God's power, for she even claimed she was a healer herself. But she couldn't make herself better. I saw her in physical pain and frustration then. And I believe God had seen her pain and frustration too. **God gave me an informed word: "She wouldn't get healed if you don't pray**." As I was alerted, I complied, and the Lord God healed her, because I was available to offer a prayer for her at that time. It is such a privilege not just to know God, but to be working in a place where I meet people where they are. And God, He is so good to all.

And today, the 1st of December 2020, Dawn, the lady I prayed for back in July, came to my till again. I was just sort of asking if she was still working, and she told me she went back to work when she got healed after I prayed for her. So I Praise God for her, for what the Lord did for her. God is so Amazing, He's truly a Loving Father to us all.

On the 26th of September 2020, Saturday, there was another lady who came to my till, and before paying for her shopping said, "Thank you for praying for my husband, he's alright now."

"Oh, ah; what's wrong with him?" I asked.

"Cancer; he's alright now, thank you, thank you."

"What, ah … what's your name?" I asked.

"Marilyn," she replied, and then walked away and pointed at my next customer.

That's all I could say. I couldn't even ask her, "What do you mean, his cancer is healed?" Whether it was cancer, or it was just benign, I haven't got a clue, but that's all I can tell you. I felt embarrassed to dig in, or question her too personally, because I felt like it was intimidating. I just thank God for healing these people. I can't always remember the people I pray for; sometimes I can only journal the event after they come back and say, "Thank you." After they come back and tell me and thank me, then I normally put their experience into a journal, but sometimes I forget.

I saw her again once or twice and she told me that her husband is in remission. She explained to me, "It means he's not getting worse, but he will not get better either," she said. And I'm thinking to myself, "Surely the Lord can heal him completely. God can complete what He started of His healing him." I felt embarrassed to insist on praying more. Some people are happy with the result of one prayer, and don't want to get God too involved. I think it's because they think their life style would have to change, and no-one wants life changes.

It's God's will for us to get healed, that's why God sent His only Son. He fulfilled His agenda, spoken of by the prophets, like Isaiah. He said in the book of Isaiah, chapter 53 verse 5, that ***by His stripes*** (the Lord Jesus' physical wounds) ***we are healed***—past tense. We are already healed because of His wounds; we just need to believe Him. Whichever part of our body is hurting, whether it's in our heads or somewhere else, claim it by those wounds He received in His body on the Cross; you are healed. He did it for us. He shed His own blood for our cleansing; our consciences are cleansed through our faith in Him.

When we know we are guilty of sin, and we feel the weight of that sin in our soul—because no human persuasion can cleanse what's in our thoughts or what's in our soul—that's when we can claim the promised cleansing blood of Jesus by the outworking of the Holy Spirit in us, to make our whole conscience became free from every guilt we may be feeling. So when you go to God and confess your sin, it says that *He is faithful and just to forgive us our sins, and to cleanse us from all unrighteousness,* see 1 John 1:9. How? By becoming human. Why? So that He knew what it was like to feel anguish, sorrow, anger, criticism, being misunderstood, physical pain, being bruised and eventually dying; the pain of being abandoned, betrayal by one of His disciples who was supposed to be a friend. (He ate with him, and had sweet fellowship with him.) The Lord Jesus humbly lived as a poor human being, so that He who knew no sin, could die for our inherited sins, erasing our guilty conscience by the power of His own blood that He shed on the Cross for the whole world. Not just for you and me, but for the whole wide world He created.

And we, as Christian believers now, are considered to be the ambassadors of Christ for the world through our faith in Him who put power in our hearts and spirit to deploy against the spirits in the air—our enemies (which are God's enemies too). We fight through the power of God over and above our circumstances. We also bind the enemy's spirit on earth, and loose the power of God from heaven and His Holy Spirit, according to the power the Lord Jesus invested in us that we received from Him, to demolish the work of the enemy in people's lives!

7

CHILDREN ARE PRECIOUS GIFTS FROM GOD

It was six o'clock in the morning, and my mum was busy sorting out dad with his cup of coffee and breakfast, while getting ready to take to the market what dad had caught in his night's fishing. There were always shrimps, king prawns, crabs and fish to sort out. Some fish was normally left for our food, but the prawns, shrimps and crabs, and other sort of sellable fish would be taken to the market to sell, for this was our main source of income. While on the other hand, my brothers and sisters were all busy getting ready for school; my eldest sister who was at college was busy putting her grease paint make up on and lipstick, complete with slightly skew-whiff eyeliner.

My eldest brother and second sister were both at high school. By then my eldest brother had already washed, ready for school. And my second eldest sister was busy ironing her uniform, an everyday task for her because she only had one set of uniform and an extra blouse, so she always went to school very neat, clean and tidy every day. Laziness never entered her bones, and she always washed her skirt and blouse the minute she got in from school, ready to have it dry and ironed again for the next day.

My other brother and sister were the last ones to scrub their faces and brush their teeth. At half past seven in the morning, primary school children have to be in school grounds to sing the National Anthem. All traffic and people stop whatever they're doing momentarily while the flag ceremony is taking place, in respect to our beliefs and patriotism as Filipino citizens. Then there was this little exercise regime (stretching and bending) for elementary school children, before the actual lessons began.

My brother and I, the youngest in the family, were left to play and mess about all day long. He was my little hero when we were very young; he used to tell me, "Little girl, do not cry," when I got hurt. "If you cry it will hurt even more, so don't, little girl, don't."

We seven children in the family had all different characters: One was over-acting, one was considered rebellious yet very kind to me, one didn't answer back, one was spoiled, I was a cry baby, my eldest brother was obedient, respectful and considerate, while my eldest sister loved cleaning and was conscientious. My parents must have been so patient, stretching time to look after us, and discipline us.

My mum and dad said they treated us all equally, but I noticed the young ones always had to do as they were told and had to wait for everything. They always came last concerning material needs, but in terms of food, always first. I suppose food was our basic need when we were little. While my brother and I were busy playing, dad was normally catching up on sleep, after all-night fishing—sometimes at the sea and sometimes at the river. When my brother and I got bored of playing, we would take our elder brother's and sister's schoolbooks and pretend to read. My brother would say some words that made sense in my hearing, while I was just making silly noises that didn't make sense at all, not even to me. He knew how to count to more than five, but I could only count up to four.

By half-past nine in the morning, dad would get up to see what we could have for a snack. If mum was home from the market, there would always be some sort of sweet bread. But if my mum wasn't home by then, dad used to take us to the nearest store to buy something. We were not allowed real sweets, just maybe tiny bread or peanuts in sticky sugar; quite messy but delicious, especially when you're hungry. This was our time on weekdays.

But on weekends we used to do some planting in the plot of land dad had cultivated. My two brothers, sister and I went out in the field to help dad plant anything from cassava, corn, and peanuts, to string beans and sweet potatoes. Although sometimes it was hard work for us, there was a fun time too: it was always in the afternoon when mum and dad were having their nap. We used to play hide and seek, hop scotch and my favourite game which we called 'bungle'. The leader drew a circle and placed an empty tin in the centre of that circle. Then we threw our slippers at it to knock it down. Whoever knocked it over first was the winner, but there were no winning prizes—it was just a game.

And we also used to dig up some of the plants we planted when we thought they were ready for harvest, so we could cook them and then plant the stalks back in the ground, so dad wouldn't noticed we had pulled out any plants. We got hold of big empty pineapple or sardine tins which we used for cooking corn or peanuts. We were careful not to be caught, but occasionally we were, and when Dad caught us, the four of us got smacked for it, especially when the plants were not quite ready for harvest, because all our hard work came to nothing. All the plants we pulled out were wasted. They were supposed to be our food supplement instead of buying bread for snacks.

Dad would then tell us off and punish us for it. He would tell us all to lie straight on the floor face down. I was always the last one in the queue, but while dad gave one or two smacks to each of them, I was already crying (as if I felt their pain), and when it was my turn, dad always told me to get up, still crying, so I always missed the smacking pains on the backside. But I was the one who cried the most. I wasn't only crying a lot fearing I would get smacked, but I felt so sorry for my elder brother, because he always got smacked the most; but they only cried a bit.

Being the youngest in the family and obedient, so dad used to say (though I was the last one to lie down on the floor face down—that was being obedient in dad's eyes), it would stop me from being smacked. Only once did I remember being smacked for carrying on crying. I was about eight years old, and dad said, "Now you've got a reason to cry."

One of my brothers used to put cardboard under his shorts to alleviate the smacking pains, but it didn't always work.

So we grew up knowing that discipline and obedience were essential to our up-bringing and no one escaped it. In a way I was thankful for my parents' disciplining us. I am glad there are still parents who agree to discipline their children. If you have never been disciplined by your parents, you are not truly loved by them. Discipline is a warning, to avoid any bad consequences against the law and punishment.

8

MY TEENAGE YEARS

The sound of people's laughter on the busy streets of December nights, lighted by the moonbeam, was exciting and transformed the people's hearts and minds. This season of midnight mass, as we called it, was a truly fantastic time for us in the city (my home county became a city in the 1970's). I don't know if midnight mass was happening in other parts of the country, but it was in my town. As we walked along the streets on our way to the church, the moon was so big and bright that it served as a light on our way there; it truly did shine like daylight above us all. With the cloudless blue sky, so blue, and the glittering stars above us, and the cool breeze that gently caressed our faces and hair—it was so refreshing. As we walked and laughed and talked, and bantered with our companions on our way to church it really did make us all feel so good to be alive. And just to be out there with our friends and families with one purpose in mind: to experience that excitement of walking under the open blue sky and the brightness of a big moon; oh, it was like being in a dream. Midnight mass was just an excuse to go out there. They were different kinds of nights altogether, and—with the throng of noisy and excited crowds, as happy as they can be—it was an occasion we celebrated year after year. We didn't walk with other people like that at other times of year, so we were always looking forward to those happy December nights. It made us all feel so joyful and alive to be participating in this happy occasion, with friendly crowds everywhere you turn, people smiling and joking with us and talking with us. And I was one of these excited people, walking with my sister and a friend, rushing to go church to attend this midnight mass.

Wherever we looked, everybody's faces were happy. Actually, it was not just the midnight mass itself that made us excited, but the crowds of happy people walking with us, and the freedom of experiencing being with the excitement of joyous crowds, and the glittering stars and the moon so big and bright as if looking down on us with a great big smile on its face. It was almost like a dream for us children; such a fantastic feeling! We all had one purpose: to walk to church and to engage in conversations and laughter, and to share the excitement with our friends and family on our way there, and to eat some warm food afterwards. No other excitement could I compare to this when I was little. No-one ever looked depressed—everyone was so happy. It was just simply an amazing feeling! I can almost feel it in my soul right now. It made me feel so free, and safe; we knew we were all safe.

The courting between young ladies and young men normally started in those days, with young people eyeing up each other (my older brother included; I saw him once with a friend or a girlfriend and he told me off for saying hi to him. "What are you doing here?" he said), and young men checking out which girls they could walk home with later on that night.

This midnight mass was celebrated year after year, which normally falls between the first and the second week of December until Christmas Eve. Whether midnight mass was one of the traditions handed down to us by the Spaniards as they colonised our country for over three hundred years I do not know, but Roman Catholicism was, and still is, embraced by Filipinos everywhere; regarded as one of the best religions ever founded then, but I thank God He opened our eyes to a relationship with the Lord Jesus and the Holy Spirit. God loosed us out of religion, praise God.

During this season, the church was always packed with people from all walks of life. I sensed the unity and happiness in the people's faces; just being in the crowd of these people made me feel a part of this joyous midnight December event.

Even the coastguards were caught up with all the excitement that midnight mass could bring. They used to drive to and fro along the streets where the crowds were. Although they were supposed to be on duty and the coast was miles away from the church, they would drive up and round a few times a week. Maybe they just wanted to be a part of the people's excitement.

This was the night I remembered quite vividly about midnight mass. It was my thirteenth birthday. My sister, our friend, and I were walking along to go to church like everybody else; but I didn't really want to walk on that night as I felt lazy, but we carried on walking. I didn't want to appear such a moaner; it was the first time I had gone out at night without adult supervision. Oh the cool breeze that was sweeping through my face and hair, with the glowing brightness of the moonlight that served as a light on our way to church, I was as excited as any human being could be, and as free as my sister and our friend felt. No mums or any grown up could tell us, "Don't do this and don't do that" and "You have to go home now." But it was about five to six miles there and back and some part of the fields and some houses were dark, as the shadows of the tree blocked them out.

There wasn't much public transport about, and we couldn't probably afford transport anyway. I was wishing somebody would give us a lift, but that was impossible, as only the coastguards drive through the streets. Everybody wanted to walk and the roads were clear. Nobody gave lifts to anyone or were even driving through the streets. Walking to church where the uninterrupted moonlight lighted our way to church was that midnight mass passion. Because walking at night with the throng of people made it more exciting than using any vehicle, but I just felt lazy. A few minutes later the coast guards' jeep stopped next to us and asked us if we wanted a lift. "My birthday present," I silently said to myself. "Yes please," we replied and climbed in the seats excitedly and off to church we went. As we were leaving and thanking the men for the lift, they shouted to us, "Don't forget the handsome coast guards." "We won't," we replied, not meaning it. After all, we were only children and didn't care whether they were handsome or not.

We had attended the midnight mass many years but that was the only time we got a lift from the coastguards on my thirteenth birthday. Sometimes we heard some people asking these coastguards for a lift to church (jokingly anyway) but they would refuse them, because they were not allowed to do so, anyway. Apart from being on duty, they were not allowed to give anyone a lift, unless it was something to do with the coast guards' rescue operation. One of my uncles was working in their office at that time; he was one of the senior officers in the coastguards unit, so we knew they shouldn't have given us the lift, but we were grateful. Well, it might just be a pure coincidence, but I got my wish on that night, on my thirteenth birthday. That was the last time I remember attending the midnight mass.

My eldest brother used to tease us when he heard us asking mum's permission to attend the evening mass. He told mum we were not really interested in attending the church service, we were one of those 'winnowing basket worshippers', and he would laugh at us. It meant we were just pretending to attend the evening mass. We were really there to buy food from the ladies, who sold some palatable snacks, neatly arranged in their (round shaped and open) winnowing baskets. He knew there was food for sale during the midnight mass, outside the church gates by the roadside, and almost everybody was flocking to the streets to buy something to eat before they went back home, but we were actually caught up with the excitement of being with the crowd of people. We didn't have money to buy anything; it was very rare that we could afford anything.

But oh, there was this warming drink, that made you sweat and refreshed you, made from bashed ginger boiled in water and sugar. You may think it sounds 'yuck' but it actually tastes good with *puto bongbong*. It's ground rice with coconut milk, sugar and other ingredients cooked inside a little bamboo tube; it's delicious with this hot ginger drink.

During and after this midnight mass season, there was also a fairground attraction, which was a fun thing to do when you're quite young because you could actually win a prize; from a set of drinking glasses to a tin of biscuits, big bottles of drinks or toys etc. We would watch these men dressed up as women to perform their dances and sing song routines, with their names changed to sound westernised; those gimmicky ones such as Carla B. Jones.

The fun thing was when we bought tickets and waited for those lady-men to do their performing acts, and then see the wooden jockey and carousel to circle round the pretend arena and we actually won a prize.

I was also in this fairground place when I accidentally trod on a piece of a broken bottle. I cut my foot quite deep and it was bleeding badly. My sister and brother were so frightened that they didn't know what to do. They thought they would be told off but it was not their fault. My brother four years older than me ran home and called mum to take me home and help me. We did not have money to take me to hospital or get us transport home. My mum could not bandage my foot until we got home because the pressure when I was walking made it worse. My siblings kept on asking if I was okay, and mum asked me if I was feeling faint. I said I was fine. I wasn't even frightened, though I cried a bit the first time I saw how big the cut was, and I didn't feel any pain at all. I don't know how long it was before it got better.

Even at this young age I felt God was with me. The peace in my heart I felt then was the same peace I know now. I know now that it was the Holy Spirit's peace.

9

DREAMS AND VISIONS

In the early stage of my pregnancy, I had a dream. In my dream I saw the Lord Jesus and some ladies with Him who looked like Israelites ladies, wearing old fashion clothing, as you would see in Bible times. I was sitting on steps near a dilapidated building. In this dream the Lord Jesus was holding in His hand bunches of flowers. And those ladies were snatching the flowers off His hand. I said to myself, "I am not going to do that, it's rude to snatch away flowers from Him." But the Lord Jesus was just happy, playing and almost teasing with them to see who could take away the bunches out of His hands. All of a sudden, they all disappeared. Looking down on my left, I saw a bunch of beautiful flowers that were left at the bottom side of the steps I was sitting on. I said to myself, "Is this for me?" But because there was no-one to answer my question, I didn't pick up the flowers, and I left them there to see what was going to happen to them. I looked away, then tried to see if anyone was coming to pick up the flowers, but then the flowers disappeared. I was so upset, crying and really blaming myself for not collecting the bunch of flowers that was left behind. As I was sitting there really remorseful, a single flower dropped onto my lap. I picked it up and looked at it, and it was a bit scorched on the petals. I was unhappy that it was not as beautiful as the bunch of flowers that was left beside me. Then I stared at this single carnation and it became beautiful on its own, I smiled to myself in the end seeing this single carnation become beautiful on its own.

Years passed, and one time as I was reading a book called *Good Morning Holy Spirit*, I noticed that the mother of the author also had a dream of a rose when she was pregnant with him. And I realised that flowers signified children in her dream. And so I know that this single carnation in my dream meant that I would only have one child, because I didn't desire to have more than one child (that bunch of flowers). So this child the Lord gave me, represented by a carnation, is now an adult; and I'm so grateful the Lord gave her to me. So I thank You, Lord Jesus. Amen.

It was the 16th July 2003 and I had, I believe, a Godly dream. In my dream I was inside the grounds of a castle, or maybe a mansion, and just by the entrance I saw a family. I saw them playing together and smiling, happily enjoying themselves, not bothering to go inside the castle or mansion. Just like them, I wasn't bothering to see what was inside the castle either. Then they stopped and read some sort of leaflet. They were just lying, resting on the ground as one would in the same situation, enjoying themselves on this summer day. I was wondering what I was doing in this castle ground alone. I wasn't bored or unhappy or looking for company; I just felt happy, relaxed and contented. (This castle or mansion was like a tourist place where people could visit and explore. But I and the family weren't doing that.) I glanced at the other side of this ground and beside me was a puppy with the sweetest smile on its face and a lion cub with a friendly smile on its face too. They were playing together as though they were very good friends. This puppy had a constant smile on its face and all the time looked so happy. And this baby lion was just happily sitting about and playing with this little dog.

I looked at the family and they were about to leave.

Then I heard a voice speak to me and say, **"The dog will talk to you when that family leaves."** Then as I looked at this puppy, who had a doggie smile on its face, so sweet, rubbing itself on this baby lion and it told me, **"Lisa is …"** and mumbled. Knowing it was a dog I couldn't say "pardon me" or ask it to repeat what he said. I thought to myself in my dream, *I just have to wait for this puppy to speak again.* Then the puppy transferred itself on the other side of this baby lion, still with a sweet doggie smile on its face, and again he said, "Lisa is …" and it mumbled again. I just didn't quite catch what this puppy said.

Then I woke up. (I know without a shadow of the doubt that it was not just an ordinary dream; my heart was beating faster.) Then I asked the Lord, "Lisa is … what? my Lord." And the **Lord answered and said, "Lukewarm."** I clasped my hand over my mouth and said, "Lukewarm, my Lord?" The Lord repeated what He said, "Lukewarm."

I stopped and thought to myself, *O my God, what can I do?* In my mind I was thinking, *She goes to church with us, she's fine*, but I cannot deny what I heard directly from the Lord, that she's lukewarm. Because the Lord said she was, I know that it's definitely true.

"O my Lord!" I exclaimed, "What can I do to help her?" And I felt the Lord was encouraging me to fast. "O my God, it's so difficult to fast. And how long can I fast?" I was contemplating within myself how long would be the most acceptable time to fast—maybe about three days, I'm thinking, or a day—but this is such a grievous problem in my daughter's walk with God. I was worried.

One day is not enough, maybe three days. As I was contemplating how many days was an acceptable time to fast, I heard the Lord say to me, **"Seven days, to cover**

the days of the week, so the enemy could not get her." "Thank you, Lord," I whispered.

In response to the Lord I said, "O my Lord, help me." So then and there I decided I would fast, starting on that day for seven days, as I heard the Lord give me the thought.

On the first day of my fast, after Lisa left for school, I went to her room, knelt by the side of her bed and read the Bible for a long time. And just before she came home from school as I was praying in the toilet, **I saw a vision of the Lord Jesus sitting on her bed waiting for her to come home.** I said to the Lord, "Shall I go and see You there in Lisa's bedroom?" The Lord didn't yes, and He didn't say no either, so I had a quick peek in her room, and **I saw a dip left in her bed, a mark where I saw the Lord sit.**

In the evening I told my Lisa the dream the Lord gave me about her. I said, "Oh darling, the Lord told me that you are lukewarm." I can't remember her actual response, but I do remember she told me of visions she had. But I know the Lord sees her heart.

The first one my Lisa told me today, July 16, 2003 (my first day of fasting). She said her visions happened around January 2003, so the beginning of that year, but she had kept them to herself. The reality is she was very frightened to be known as a Christian by the other children, especially the boys at her school. We had moved our Sunday church service to this school about ten months before I had this dream, though I heard her telling me, maybe once, that she didn't want to be known as a Christian any more—not in her school. She was scared she might get bullied by other children. She was very apprehensive to let other children know she was a Christian, although a couple of her friends knew she was. She invited them to church, and one came and accepted the Lord as her Saviour.

And this is how her visions came about. She told me that one evening she couldn't go to sleep. So she made herself tired by going to bed very late and doing some of the things she normally does in the morning before going to school. (That's why I sometimes heard her tinkering about late at night.) She was scared, and thought about all sorts of bad things in her mind, but she wasn't letting me know about her fears. She knew she was not fully asleep but not fully awake either; she was just lying in her bed and she knew it was not just a dream.

In her vision she saw lots of huge mountains. At the foot of these mountains were lots and lots of little demons, frightening and teasing, taunting and scaring her. She rebuked these demons but they didn't go away. She was very, very scared and she was crying. She wanted to get up but her body just felt so heavy. She wanted to move but she couldn't. She tried calling out for me, "Mum!" but no voice came out of her mouth. She then rebuked the demons again, still feeling very scared, but she couldn't make these demons go away.

Then suddenly she saw the right Arm of God overshadowing the mountains (she told me God's arm was huge), and those little demons who were taunting her just sunk into the earth and died, and others were banished away. All of these demons were absolutely terrified of God's Arm.

What I saw in her situation was that she fought and fought and when she couldn't do anything more, the Lord fought for her and rescued her from these frightening sights of demons. After seeing **the Arm of the Lord causing these demons to disappear and die**, she said she felt at peace and then had peaceful sleep. And when she woke up in that morning, she didn't feel tired and wasn't scared any more. So I thank God the

Lord rescued her. This one was a true vision she had in January 2003 when she was awake.

In her second vision—she called it a dream this time—again she was lying in her bed. It was a few weeks back, so it was about near the end of June or maybe beginning of July 2003—so maybe it was the same month of that year when the Lord told me she was lukewarm.

So here she told me her second vision. She said she was in the field at King Harold School, wearing her Mackenzie hooded cardigan, which was one of her favourite items of clothing (she thinks it was the latest fashion that year), and blue jeans. She was about fifteen years old, and this is how she saw herself: She was kneeling and praying alone in the school grounds, when all of a sudden **she saw lots and lots of souls going up to heaven**. Then she saw her own soul going up to heaven as well, but she tugged hard at it—she didn't want her soul to go up, so she shouted "No!" But her soul went up anyway, then she woke up.

As a mother I was thoroughly relieved to know that her soul went up to heaven too. And in November that year, 2003, at the age of 15, my Lisa decided to be baptised in water. Hearing her saying she saw her own soul going up to heaven and she tugged on it, makes me think: When the Lord said in my dream, she was lukewarm, it truly makes sense to me. I was thinking that because she went along to church with us, she must be on fire with God; but God knew her heart.

And today, the 11th of February 2020, in the very early hours of the morning, I had a dream where I was lying on top of the bed, with a creamy-colour cotton bed spread, and I saw the Lord Jesus draw a line on the left side of the bed I was lying on (the right side of my body), and then on the right side of the bed (the left side of my body and just below my feet) where I was lying on, and then I saw the Lord do something in my head, touching my hair, but I didn't feel His touch. I just saw the Lord Jesus leaning over me, touching my head so lovingly. I was sweating and I looked ill, as if I was in pain. The first time I saw Him, I didn't quite get what the Lord was doing over my head. Then I realised it was like soothing my pain, but I couldn't feel His hand on me. I awoke with the horrendous sounds of the stormy wind and a very heavy rain. I felt slightly worried about our garden fence.

In reality the night before there was a bad storms warning in Great Britain. There were yellow warnings everywhere. (I have lived here for nearly 34 years and I have never seen a weather warning like that before, with yellow warnings all over Britain.) As the strong gusts of wind and rain woke me up, the moment I was aware of it, I prayed. The minute I said "Amen," the strong gusts of wind and blowing rain completely stopped. (I checked the time and it was 2:59 a.m.in the morning.)

I found out that on that morning my husband had been woken up by this strong gust of wind and heavy rain too, and he had prayed at the same time, and he said exactly the same things happened: He noticed that the minute he said "Amen," the blowing gust of wind and rain stopped completely. We were both worried that our fence might be blown down or any disruption may occur. But thank God it was all fine. He said, "Yes, the gust of winds and the rain stopped immediately after I prayed." That's what I noticed too, so we were woken up with this storm at the same time and prayed exactly at the same time and the stormed stopped immediately. Praise God.

After praying that the storms would stop, and they

did, I asked the Lord what my dream meant. And the Lord reminded me of the scripture from the book of Job, chapter 38, verses 8–11, when He marked off the sea, and He said, ***'This far you may come and no farther; here is where your proud waves halt.'*** So it means no harm will come very near me; only as far as the Lord Jesus has put these lines or this barrier beside me, and no further, so it would not reach me. *This far you should go and no further*. Amen and praise you, O LORD GOD ALMIGHTY.

In the early hours of this morning, Monday the 10th of August 2020 at 4:20 am, I was praying. The news of this coronavirus was looming in the air, and all over the world people needed to segregate themselves from each other; with the effect that our church meeting is now on line, a virtual Sunday morning service, and schools in Britain are closed. Even restaurants and cinemas and other public places are closed. I was asking the Lord what is going to happen to the future of the church and would this be the start of a new church. I felt the Lord remind me of the word I'd seen on New Year's Eve: the word 'Ended'.

I reminded one of the leaders in our church that I sent him a text on the 5th of January 2020, about the word 'Ended'. The meaning of it is: Whatever is going to happen will happen; the Lord will not stop anything though He has power to do it. But those real Christians, Christian to the core, if they call on God they will be safe; but the unbelievers will not be so safe.

It's like the Lord has stopped intervening to show His love to the world. If we stop praying, all things that are going to happen will happen. And at that time, the 5th of January 2020, I had never heard of any news about this coronavirus, and here it is after ten weeks or so. Life has completely changed all over the world, when we did not see this coming! And today, mid-March, the coronavirus is looming.

The second thing the Lord reminded me today, Monday the 23rd of March 2020, was the word I heard when I was in a church service, back on the 7th of October 2018. As we were worshipping, I felt the Lord wanted me to be silent and listen to Him for a while, so I did. And this is what I heard: **"Islamisation will increase" and that "anyone who wanted to write a book should do it within three years (it means up to 2021). In three years we would see quite a lot of Muslim people, even in Waltham Abbey. In five years they would be spreading about everywhere, and we would even see them in the street of our church, and in seven years we will be swamped by them, and there will be a Muslim prime minister in Britain."** In reality, on that very week when the Lord informed me of this, I saw four people inside the shop where I worked, women and children, wearing the hijab. That evening on BBC news I saw Teresa May going inside 10 Downing Street followed by a man in white Muslim attire, which I had never seen on the television before, only after the Lord informed me did I see such a sight.

And today is the 23rd of March 2020, nearly two years ago when I heard the Lord say, "**Islamisation will rise in Britain," during that worship time in the church.** But now I heard the Lord telling me this morning, **"Britain will be gone to the dogs!"** When all these things happen, watch out—**Britain will be gone to the dogs.**

For a few days now this dream I had on the 11th of Feb. 2020 keeps on coming back to me and today, the 9th of August 2020, Sunday, I was wondering: what does it really mean? Why would the Lord draw a line on my right and on my left and just below my feet on the bed I was lying on? I clearly remember the Lord Jesus leaning His head towards mine, lovingly touching my very dark hair (that's how I remembered it), looking at my face, as if He saw me suffering. In this dream I didn't really want the Lord to feel the sweat on my head because I was feeling embarrassed that my head was sweating, as if I was very ill.

I was really wondering, *what does this dream mean?* then. And today a first thought came to mind as I was having a shower. The main leader in the healing rooms where I was working (still does on-line occasionally) told me all of them except one who attended the regional meeting had Covid19. She said they didn't know what they had at that time with the symptoms, then they realised they all had Covid19. Also, a friend of mine told me she had mild symptoms of Covid19 a few months back. She experienced shortness of breath at night time, feeling really awful and weak. As their words reverberate through my mind I feel the Lord reminded me of my dream about my lying in bed and the Lord putting a line on both sides of my bed and one below my feet, as he leant over my head touching my hair, but I didn't feel His hands.

And the meaning at that time—the seas pounding waves will halt at the line the Lord places—is the personal revelation that the Lord protected me from Covid19, so not to be touched by the pandemic that was looming in those early months of this year. I realised that when the Lord showed me this in my dream, it was about the same time I didn't attend the regional meeting I was invited to go to. And the whole revelation that the Lord placed a line indicated thus far it would go and no further, was a true blessing. The Lord protected me against Covid19—it will not come near me. The only difference I felt during this pandemic was my eyes felt itchy occasionally, which I have never felt before.

After the Lord's revelation, I felt so grateful for the Lord Jesus' total protection. O my God, thank you, Lord Jesus. And if the Lord had not protected me from the pandemic, I would not be able to tell the story of my mum, and others stories through dreams and visions the Lord revealed to me in the past. It really wouldn't make any sense to an unbeliever, and it might even sound weird to other Christians, but I know what revelation I received, and truly, if you're saying you're a Christian believer and never had any experience of the work of God in your life, how could you say, you believe? If you are Christian and connected to God in the spirit He gave you, you would have Godly experiences, even just a few.

Some people might say I'm just making it all up, but I couldn't make up my dreams. I even had a dream a few years back that one of my colleagues, a man, was going to have a baby. Two months later after my dreams, he—not personally him—and his girlfriend had their first baby girl. She looks like him, she's so cute.

10

THIS TIME MY DREAM BECOMES REALITY

It was April 2013 and David my husband had booked a holiday for us to go Fuerteventura. But for a few weeks I was worried about going away; there was the news that some people who went abroad died; some of them got mobbed or became very ill abroad and they didn't manage to come home; that thought terrified me. Then I would rebuke my own thoughts, and declare that the protection of the Lord is upon us, His people. All these negative thoughts had a hold on me, and I was thinking, *How about if I die abroad? What was David going to do and say, how about if David died abroad?—what was I going to do? How could I go home, and what would I say to his family?* All these sorts of negative feelings and thoughts went through my head. And I was scared stiff at the thought of all these bad things. I know these were such bad thoughts, and I shouldn't even write them down, but that was what was going on my head. I thank God the Lord even knew my worries.

My daughter kept on asking us, "Why don't you go on holiday abroad? Why is it always in the U.K.?" When I mentioned to her about the news I heard, she told me off saying, "Mum, you're a Christian; why are you so scared? Mum, you keep on telling me that God looks after His people? Just go on, book your holiday anywhere, to Lanzarote, it's nice there." She had been there with her boyfriend's family, and she thoroughly enjoyed it.

So when David booked that holiday in Fuerteventura,

I didn't tell him about my worries as I didn't want him to worry as well. On the evening of our flight I couldn't go to sleep as all these bad thoughts wearied me. I kept on praying and rebuking all the horrible thoughts, but they wouldn't go away. We went to bed at eight o'clock but at ten o'clock I was still awake. After lying in bed for what seemed such a long time, I eventually fell asleep. I woke up at midnight to go to the toilet and went back to bed, feeling really tired and unrested; not just my body but my mind too.

Eventually I got back to sleep, and on that very evening before we flew to Fuerteventura, I had a short dream. In this dream I was inside my house and there were quite a lot people outside the door who all wanted to come in; two particular men that I know so well were so insistent on coming into my house. It seemed to be my home, but it was definitely different from the appearance of my real home. I just kept on refusing them to enter the house; I told them, "No, you cannot come in." Even others were hanging around to come in, but I managed to stop them all from entering my house.

The scene changes and now I saw myself in dreams praying, "Lord, I send the Angels to Fuerteventura to protect us." As I was saying these things in my dream, my mind interrupted me, reiterating, *It's not my Angels, it's God's Angels.* So even in my dreams I had the consciousness they are God's Angels, and that I couldn't just send any Angel, for I do not have any authority nor the right to send any of them anywhere; they're God's Angels, not mine. So I changed my prayer to, "Lord, I'm praying, O my God, that You would send Your Angel, ahead of us to Fuerteventura to protect us and to guide us and keep us safe, wherever we are going; before we leave our home. Lord Jesus, that You, O My God, will send Your Angel in the aeroplane, in the hotel, and even in the taxi, Lord. And that no spirit that is not of You, Lord Jesus, will attach to us in the place where we are going; in Jesus' Name, Amen." This is how my prayer went in my dreams, and then I woke up.

Our flight was scheduled to leave at six o'clock that morning, so we needed to be in the airport by four o'clock. But when we woke up, I told David, "Love, we have to pray." I hadn't finished speaking, when he said, "We do not have the time for that." So I told him my dreams and he agreed that we needed to pray. So then I repeated all the prayers I had prayed for in my dreams—protection before we even leave home, in the airport, Fuerteventura itself, in the hotel where we were staying, and that no spirit that is not of the Lord would attach to us, and even in the taxi. "Lord, Your Angel be with us. You will send Your Angel ahead of us to protect and guide wherever we're going, in Jesus' Name, Amen."

The taxi driver was booked to pick us up at 4 a.m. He came ten minutes early. David opened the door when he knocked, and I had a quick peek outside and saw a man standing there, waiting for the taxi driver to finish putting our luggage in the boot of the car. As David was locking the door behind us, I quietly told him, "Oh, there's a man with him," but I don't think David heard me. This man I saw had a white long-sleeve shirt and dark trousers. I was taken aback, thinking, *Why did this taxi driver have a man with him?* I was thinking to myself, *I can't say anything to this taxi man—it's not my taxi.* I thought to myself, *Where is he going to sit? Were we both going to sit at the back of the taxi, or will David sit next to the driver, and this man will sit next to me?* As I was thinking this before we got into the taxi, a swift white vehicle drove past and the man that was standing there a minute or so before completely disappeared. I said, "Lord what does this mean?" And I heard the Lord reply, **"The Angel, you prayed, remember?"** I was so excited at the back of the car thanking God for the Angel He sent to go ahead of us, to protect us.

When we got out of the taxi, I said to David, "Love, did you see the man that was standing there waiting for the taxi driver to leave?"

"No," he said.

"Oh, did you see the swift white vehicle, the long one, that drove past just before we got in the taxi?"

He said, "No car could drive past the taxi, as it was parked in the middle of the road."

I was so excited I said to him, "Ok, I'll tell you a secret: The Lord sent an Angel with the taxi driver. I saw him standing there waiting for the driver to finish loading our luggage in the boot. He disappeared when this white swift vehicle passed by. He was just like an ordinary-looking man, wearing a white shirt and dark trousers. Then I explained to him, **"The Lord told me that the man who was standing there before we crossed the road was an Angel.** The Lord reminded me of my prayer and said, **'Remember you prayed.'**"

I was so happy, excited and felt really at peace. Thank YOU, Lord Jesus. So I feel that my dream became reality, for the Lord answered my prayers then and there, as I saw the Angel of the Lord standing there waiting for us to leave home. It just reminded me that when I prayed that the Lord would send His Angel ahead of us, God's Angel went just before we crossed over the road to his swift car, as we were getting into the taxi.

When we were actually in Fuerteventura, I heard a voice of a man as we were walking on the streets, in the market area. He called out to me and said, "Amigo, amigo" which means *friend, friend*. But I didn't turn around to look at him as I was a bit scared that he might stop us. When I heard that voice, I felt the Lord was telling me that he was an Angel. But I wasn't sure if it just in my thoughts, or if it was really an Angel the Lord sent for us. After we passed by, another man sitting on the opposite side the road when I heard the voice called to David and talked about his camera, and I was scared that he might take the camera. But obviously he was just talking, and he saw too that I was scared, and he let us go. When I reached the hotel we were staying at, I felt so remorseful thinking I ignored the Angel of the Lord He had sent for us. David heard the man too calling out to us saying, "Amigo, amigo," but he didn't look either. The way the voice said, amigo, amigo, was different from a normal person that just wanted to get one's attention. He wasn't shouting; it was actually quite a soft and long tone. The sound of that voice haunted me for a while.

I was so remorseful for not looking at the man who said, "Amigo, amigo." It was also on the same day that we crossed over to Lanzarote from Fuerteventura on a small glass-bottom boat. The sea was a bit rough, and on the way back from Lanzarote, just before we boarded that boat, I saw a quick glimpse of a swift creamy white object that just went ahead of me as we were boarding. I believe the Lord God was trying to tell me that He was with me, even on the Atlantic Ocean. I thank You, Lord Jesus.

But today as I'm writing this part of the story, I feel remorseful again, and am sorry that I didn't even thank the Angel that the Lord sent to protect and guide us, and make us feel at peace. O LORD GOD, MY LORD, FORGIVE ME, I'M SO SORRY, MY LORD GOD, for not turning around to speak to that man (YOUR Angel) that called us *Amigo*.

So my dreams became reality as I saw the Angel of the Lord standing by just before we got into the taxi. Then the swift white vehicle with the Angel disappeared from my sight.

11

ONCE SAVED ALWAYS SAVED

Ladies and gentlemen, boys and girls, good morning! Welcome to our religion class and a new topic. Today we have a timely discussion about, 'Once Saved Always Saved'.

"Oh no, here we go again," Samantha piped up. "What does it mean Miss? Is this a Christian talk again?"

"Ah … well, it is as you say, Samantha; remember this is religion class, for the well-being of our souls."

"Oh, ok, but what it is?" Samantha continued. She really wanted to know what it meant to be saved. "What does it mean 'Once saved always saved', Miss?"

Peter, bless him; he raised his hands so high and shouted, "I know Miss, I know!"

"Okay, what is it Peter? Explain it to the class."

"Well, you see," Peter started, "my mum and dad go to church every Sunday and I'm always dragged along; I'd rather play games on my phone all day long, but they wouldn't allow me. So I have to sit and listen to this man who talks and talks and talks. and sometimes we sing songs too." And he started singing "We'll give the glory to Jesus because of His love, His wonderful love. We'll give all the glory to Jesus because of His wonderful Love!"

"Get to the point Peter," interrupted Miss.

"Well, I heard this man say, 'You have to repent and accept Jesus Christ of Nazareth as your Saviour and the Holy Spirit to be saved,' and then he got this book he called the Holy Bible and read from it: 'John 3:16: *For*

God so loved the world that He gave His one and only begotten Son that whosoever believe in Him shall not perish but have everlasting life.'"

"Well done Peter."

"Thank you, Miss. It means, Miss, when we say this prayer (they called it prayer of repentance) and welcome the Lord Jesus into our hearts, to be our Lord and Saviour, we are saved. We are saved—it means we will not go to hell when we die."

A few children gasped, "Oh, what is hell?"

Kevin shouted out, "It's a hot place! That man that talked and talked and talked in the church said, 'You wouldn't want to be there, the people in there burn continuously, and they are all in agony, they're in pain.' It's an exhausting thing to explain even to an adult, let alone to a child, but I get it Miss, I get it, I understand it. As Peter already said, you need to repent and welcome Jesus and the Holy Spirit of the Living God into your heart!"

"Ok class, sit down. Well said boys, well done; thank you."

"Ah … what?" Clare gasped, "I don't want to be in hell, Miss." She paused then she said, "When is this all going to happen Miss, and what do we need to do? I've seen this movie called *Left Behind* and some people didn't manage to go to heaven—they were left behind in such chaos. And then my dad kept on saying, 'There is no God.' He doesn't believe in God but he watched the film *God Is Not Dead part 2* with his mates. I think he's changed his mind."

And Sheila now started, "When are these things going to happen, Miss? When would we know it?"

Now all the children were a bit confused and panicky: "Are we going to heaven or to hell, Miss?"

"Ok class, sit down. Are you all listening?" It is quite

true what Peter and Kevin told us, but it won't be in this natural body we have."

"And what body is it Miss? It's just so complicated!" Tom disgustedly stomped his feet.

Some ladies and a few gentlemen raised their eyes and eyebrows up, put their hands on their heads, frustrated and wanted to walk out. But the lady speaker (the Miss) warned them, "If you walk out now you will never hear the end of what Peter and Kevin have started.

"To give you an idea let's read this parable in Luke 16:19–26. Open your Bibles. Who wants to read it?"

A grown-up man stood up and started reading, "*There was a rich man who was dressed in purple and fine linen and lived in luxury every day. At his gate was laid a beggar named Lazarus, covered with sores and longing to eat what fell from the rich man's table. Even the dogs came and licked his sores. The time came when the beggar died and the angels carried him to Abraham's side. The rich man also died and was buried. In Hades…*"

"Let's stop here for a while. Hades means hell," she explained to the children; she nodded to the man and said, "Continue."

"*In Hades, where he was in torment, he looked up and saw Abraham far away, with Lazarus by his side. So he called to him, 'Father Abraham, have pity on me and send Lazarus to dip the tip of his finger in water and cool my tongue, because I am in agony in this fire.' But Abraham replied, 'Son, remember that in your lifetime you received your good things, while Lazarus received bad things, but now he is comforted here and you are in agony. And besides all this,* ***between us and you a great chasm has been set in place, so that those who want to go from here to you cannot, nor can anyone cross over from there to us****.'*" The man sat down.

"So it means when Lazarus and the rich man died, they all had real bodies in heaven and hell, when they were with Abraham, but not like the bodies we have now; for their natural bodies, like we have, were buried in the ground."

Sofia frowned, "Miss what kind of bodies do they have?"

Camilla in her posh accent retorted, "Miss, does that mean God doesn't want people to be rich?"

"Not at all Camilla, not at all class; God loves people and He gives people wealth, honour and riches. Like King Solomon, whom God gave knowledge, wisdom, honour and wealth, see 1 Kings 3:11–13. And in Job 42:10, God gave Job twice as much wealth as he had before the testing. But in this parable the rich man does not have any compassion on Lazarus, even though he had plenty to share. He didn't give him anything; not even a piece of bread! And so he suffered much in hell, but in his arrogance he thought he could still dictate to Father Abraham to tell Lazarus what to do for him. He even expected Lazarus to dip the tip of his finger in water to cool his tongue! But Father Abraham said they cannot cross over into each other territories."

"Who fixed the chasm between them Miss?"

"God, she replied, for no-one can do it apart from God!"

Miss continued, "When they were both alive in this body, like the body we have on earth, the rich man did not help Lazarus at all, and now in hell this rich man still had the mind-set that Lazarus was not as important as him, because he thought his riches on earth made him superior. He thought because he was wealthy, he was good, but his wealth became his god, and he thought he could just tell Lazarus what to do for him, even when they were both physically dead. But father Abraham would not let this rich man's attitude prevail.

"While on earth, this rich man probably threw meat on bones to his dog, and watched Lazarus eyes—almost pleading to give that bone to him instead. But now Lazarus was resting in heaven with father Abraham, being comforted his soul was at peace in heaven, while the rich man was in torment in the fire of hell. This rich man loved getting his own way, but failed.

"You see, money (wealth) cannot buy everything on earth. And you know, there's not a transaction for salvation in heaven, it has to start here on earth. When physical death takes place, salvation is assured if you believe—beginning with an open heart to the Lord Jesus. And that's what you need to know for now, okay class?"

Tom scratched his head again, and whispered, "What is a parable, and how can we open our hearts?"

Miss glanced at Tom and said, "Before you go, let me answer Tom's questions. "A parable is a simple story used to illustrate moral or spiritual lessons—like the story that we just read. And opening your heart means telling the Lord Jesus what you are thinking, what's in your heart. And that's what you just did, Tom; you opened your heart to the class, by asking a question. It's like talking to your friend. It's also like praying—talking is praying."

"Thank you, Miss." Tom smiled and off they all went home.

The next week Miss arrived in the class and said, "Good morning class (this time just the children were present), today we continue with our discussions!" Miss recaps their discussion a week before and begins this time with, "The transaction started in heaven, when God the Father sent His own Son prepared to rescue all people on earth, after the first two human beings sinned. Who can tell me who are these first two people that sinned?"

"Adam and Eve, Miss," Peter shouted.

And Miss went on to tell the class of how the story of Christmas came about. "It began with the Prophets. These are the people who hear God's voice—like Isaiah, Jeremiah and even King David, who sang a song of the Christ's sufferings—who prophesied about the Messiah's birth, His death, His resurrection and even His second coming and return to earth.

"When the Lord Jesus shouted, "It is finished," His physical work on earth was over, but ours is just beginning. But if we die without asking Jesus into our lives, we forfeit the chance of having eternal life. That's why the Lord Jesus said to Nicodemus, "You must be born again, spiritual birth.

"The process of exchange started in heaven when God the Father sent His own Son, prepared after the first two human beings sinned.

"The prophets were told about The Messiah's coming, that He is the Christ of God, and even the second King of Israel (King David) explained in his writing about the Posterity of The Messiah. But it didn't happen until over four hundred years later. That's a long, long time, and the Messiah's (that's the Son of God) birth happened a long time ago. And we know the story of Christmas, when the babe in the manger was born in Bethlehem, in the midst of the Jewish community. His birth was a Supernatural birth, born to a young virgin, who was betrothed to her fiancé, Joseph. That was the name of baby Jesus' earthly father, who found out Mary His mother was pregnant with Him. So he wanted to divorce her quietly, for Joseph was a righteous man (he didn't want Mary to be put to shame) but the minute he made up his mind about his decision, an angel of the Lord spoke to him in a dream, and commanded him and confirmed to him that the child is God's Son, and he has to name Him Jesus, for this child will save His people from all the sins the whole world has committed, and it will begin in the land of Israel.

"So Joseph did not divorce her, and he took Mary as his wife. He believed that his dream was of God. They went to Bethlehem, the town of David—because he belonged to the house and line of David—to register for the Roman Census. While they were there, the baby was born in a manger. Angels appeared to the shepherds in fields nearby, the Glory of the Lord shone, and they sang, 'Glory to God in the highest heaven, and on earth peace to those on whom His favour rests.' Some time later the Magi visited the Child and His parents, bringing gifts.

"This is how the Christmas we all know, started in Bethlehem.

"Now this happened because God firmly decided He would send His Only Son to save the whole world from the deceiver, the enemy of our soul, and an enemy to God. God made a covenant with Abraham through his family line to save us. Some of Abraham's descendants failed just like all of us do. And since there was no higher and faithful person on earth ever born that God could make an oath to have a covenant with, He made an oath with Himself that He would rescue all people on earth, through His own Son, whose family line on earth were the Israelites.

"So this sweet little Baby Jesus grew up and He found favour in the sight of God and of men. After His birth no recorded information about Him was written, until He had grown up. Apart from only one recorded history about Him when He was twelve years old, when He stayed away from His parent's side. It was then that they found out that He was talking to the high priest and the teachers of the law. And they found Jesus very interesting and so knowledgeable about the things of God; a very extra ordinary young man. And we didn't hear about Him again after He reached His thirtieth birthday. He was invited to a wedding in Cana with His mother and His disciples, and there He did the first miracle by turning water into wine.

"And then everything about Him became so intrinsically exposed to the nations of the Israelites and beyond. After three years of His ministry, one of his disciples, a money bag keeper, betrayed Him into the hands of the chief priests. After His betrayal, they hanged Him on the Cross and killed Him, and with all the accusations against Him, not one single sin was found in Him, not even a word He spoke, but they still killed Him. They still beat Him up, hanged Him on the cross, killed Him, insulted Him, spat on Him, and absolutely humiliated Him, in front of the whole community. Everyone knew His history. They even took His clothing, and stabbed Him on His side after he had already died; where the sudden flow of blood and water unceasingly came out from Him.

"But you know that the first word that came out from the Lord Jesus' mouth was, 'Father, forgive them for they know not what they are doing!' Wow, what an account of forgiveness that came out of the lips of a Sinless Man; the Son of God who just cancelled all the transgressions done against Him. With His example *we* may able to forgive whoever sinned against us. You might say it was the Jews who killed their own Messiah. But Jews and Gentiles alike killed Him, for He died for the sin of the whole world; and since your life is borrowed from Him, you too are accountable for His death, otherwise you have no part in Him, and you cannot be saved.

"And on His account He's inviting you to believe the people He sent on ahead of you on earth to rescue you, which started from the prophets to His disciples, and to this day people who believe in Him, who are witnessing to you today about Him, to benefit you and make you righteous the moment you believe. His own death on the Cross is for your benefit, that your soul might be saved, so you do not have to enter into hell. For it says in John 3:16–18: *For God so loved the world that he gave his one and only Son, that whoever believes in him shall not perish but have eternal life. For God did not send his Son into the world to condemn the world, but to save the world through him. Whoever believes in him is not condemned, but whoever does not believe stands condemned already because they have not believed in the name of God's one and only Son.*

"The Lord Jesus' legacy to the whole world—His birth, death, and resurrection—bring an unbroken relationship and eternal life to those who believe in Him, and proclaim His power over themselves.

"Ok Class, dismissed. Have a nice Christmas all of you."

All the children stood up and said, "You too, Miss."

"Goodbye, class."

"Goodbye, Miss."

BACK TO THE READER! And now, we all know it is difficult for anyone to lose their salvation, but the fact is it says in the Bible to work out your salvation.

This is the truth; if you are an ordinary Christian and you are letting the Spirit of the Living God guide and lead you, and you are willing to be guided by His love (it's a joint effort, yeah?), you are saved. For in 1 John 3:9 it says: *No one who is born of God will continue to sin, because God's seed remains in them; they cannot go on sinning because they have been born of God.* In verse 3: ***All who have this hope in Him purify themselves,*** *just as He is pure. No one who lives in Him keeps on sinning*—this is in verse 6. And in verses 23 & 24: *And this is His command: to believe in the name of His Son, Jesus Christ, and to love one another as He commanded us. The one who keeps God's commands lives in Him, and He in them. And this is how we know that He lives in us:* ***We know it by the Spirit He gave us.***

The reason why we know we are going to heaven and will inherit eternal life is because we are sealed by the Spirit of the Living God, see Ephesians 4:30. God the Holy Spirit sealed us to know we belong to Father God and the Lord Jesus Christ. See also 2 Timothy 2:19: *Nevertheless, God's solid foundation stands firm, sealed with this inscription; "The Lord knows those who are His" and "Everyone who confesses the name of the Lord must turn away from wickedness."* For me it means if the seal of the Holy Spirit of God remains in you, and you are led by God the Holy Spirit, you are saved; you walk in peace with God.

What is the sign of the Holy Spirit that you are in God's care? Let me give you an example. As I mentioned earlier when I was teenager, I went to church and really enjoyed the midnight mass year after year. I was a good little Catholic girl, and yes as I said, I had religion. But when I became a born-again Christian it became a relationship. My spirit within me was renewed and I sensed the Holy Spirit coming into me one afternoon. I was kneeling and praying (I can't even remember what I was praying for) when all of a sudden I got these tongues (words unknown to me) which I did not understand in my natural mind what I was saying, but which flowed so forcefully in me, that I could not stop it. With this I had the urge to speak this tongue to my dad, who was sleeping in his bed, having his afternoon nap. In my head I was a bit scared and was thinking he might wake up and slap me for waking him up. Nevertheless, as I was led to do this, I just started talking to him, putting my hand on his head, carrying on saying these words as if I was trying to cast out a bad spirit in him. I don't know. But my dad didn't wake up while I was doing that, so I didn't get a slap. Praise God! But when he woke up, he asked my mum, "Who came to 'CONSARGA' me?" Basically, this word that dad used means to correct, rebuke or tell off.

When I was in Roman Catholicism, I never had an encounter with the Holy Spirit's power or spoke in tongues; only when I became a born-again Christian did I ever experience that. But now I had a bit of understanding of what I read when the Lord Jesus was giving His disciples instruction after his death and resurrection, saying wait for the Holy Spirit. It says in Acts 1:4: *"Do not leave Jerusalem, but wait for the gift My Father promised, which you have heard me speak about. For John baptised with water, but in a few days you will be baptised with the Holy Spirit."* And in Acts 2:1–4: *When the day of Pentecost came, they were all together in one place. Suddenly a sound like a blowing of a violent wind came from heaven and filled the whole house where they were sitting. They saw what seemed to be tongues of fire that separated and came to rest on each of them. All of them were filled with the Holy Spirit and began to speak in other tongues as the Spirit enabled them.*

In 1 Corinthians 14:22–25: *Tongues, then, are a sign, not for believers but for the unbelievers; prophecy, however, is not for unbelievers but for believers. So if the whole church come together and everyone speaks in tongues, and enquirers or unbelievers come in, will they not say that you are out of your mind?* (Since they don't understand what you are saying) *But if an unbeliever or an inquirer comes in while everyone is prophesying, they are convicted of sin and are brought under judgement by all,* ***as the secrets of their hearts are laid bare****. So they will fall down and worship God, exclaiming, "God is really among you."*

Ephesians 1:13: *In Him you also trusted, after you heard the word of truth, the gospel of your salvation; in whom also, having believed, you were sealed with the Holy Spirit of promise.* **So it is that the Holy Spirit of God sealed you and made you His own when you started to believe God and asked the Holy Spirit to guide and lead you day by day.**

The Holy Spirit is the seal the Lord has stamped you with, so that you know with full assurance that you belong to God, and He belongs to you. When you have that seal you have the anointing; it's irrevocable and also indelible—you will never be forgotten by the Lord Jesus. That's when you know you are fully saved. And for you as a normal Christian who sins now and again, when you know you've sinned, you immediately ask for God's forgiveness. It means you've examined yourself and found some fault. When you come to the Lord Jesus, He is faithful in forgiving you again and again, providing you're not doing it on purpose. You ask the Holy Spirit to clean you and you avoid going back to your old sinful ways. And then the saying 'Once saved always saved' applies to you.

We know that salvation is free and you don't need to work for your salvation. Salvation is faith in the Son of God, and belief in the death and resurrection of His Son Jesus and the work of the Holy Spirit He promised to all believers. Yet on the other hand it says that 'faith without works is dead,' which seems to be contradictory.

But the work is to work out your salvation, see Philippians 2:12. The reason for working out your salvation means it is not one way love … **God loved us; and we do not need to work for God to love us,** or need to do things for God to love us, or so that He could love us more. God being immutable has already loved us even when we were all still sinners—that is God's nature, He is love—as we read in the very famous scripture of John 3:16. So God loves you and you don't have to do any work for God to love you, or to love you even more. You are already loved, by Him—full stop!

And we need to love God back. In 2 John 1:6 it says: *And this is love: that we walk in obedience to His commands. As you have heard from the beginning, His command is that you walk in love.* (Love God first, so that He may enable you to love your neighbour as yourself—the second commandment—and fulfil all the commandments according to the Lord Jesus, see Luke 10:27.) In 2 John verses 8 & 9 it says: *Watch out that you do not lose what we have worked for* (the apostles' teaching), *<u>but that you may be rewarded fully</u>. Anyone who runs ahead and does not continue in the teaching of Christ does not have God; whoever continues in the teaching has both the Father and the Son.*

It's slightly complicated that not all who have called on the name of the Lord will be saved, even though they experienced the goodness of God and the fellowship of the Holy Spirit in them. You could never make yourself become unsaved if you are truly walking in the leading and guidance of the Spirit of God. In Romans 8:38–39: *For I am convinced that neither death nor life, neither angels nor demons, neither the present nor the future, nor any powers, neither height nor depth, nor anything else in all creation, will be able to separate us from the love of God that is in Christ Jesus our Lord.*

It is clear the Lord Jesus' work for humanity was completed on the Cross, only your own choice can separate you from God's love. But if you are trying to put Jesus back on the Cross, oh, man, you will be in big trouble in hell. His word has a warning.

But now I'm not talking about those people mentioned in 2 John 1:7 (the deceiver and the antichrist) but those who used to be God-fearing born-again believers who became so high in their own self-belief, maybe because they were leaders of a church or pastors in a big congregation, so self-absorbed that they thought, "We know God will forgive us. Whatever we do, all we need to do is ask for His forgiveness and we will be fine; we will still be saved in the end, because we prophesied, we cast out demons and healed the sick in Jesus' name." You know what? you make God's grace cheap, that you think you can play along and it would be fine in the end. Let Him not catch you in sin when He comes back.

Let me show you something in God's word that states just that, in Matthew 7:21–23: ***"Not everyone who says to me, 'Lord, Lord,' will enter the kingdom of heaven, but only the one who does the will of my Father who is in heaven. Many will say to me on that day, 'Lord, Lord, did we not prophesy in your name and in your name drive out demons and in your name perform many miracles?' Then I will tell them plainly, 'I never knew you. Away from me, you evildoers!'*** It's the Lord Jesus Himself speaking in these passages, and do you really think you could even chirp before the Living God? Woe to you man or woman, who would dare to reason out and bring charges against God. Don't these people the Lord is talking about here sound like born-again Christians? Because you could never cast out demons etc. if you haven't been enlightened and never experienced the Holy Spirit and the goodness of God.

You could never do the work the disciples did, or even pray for the sick and they recovered. Help us, God, not to be arrogant.

You know why I'm saying these people are Christian believers? Because the Lord Jesus mentioned that you will receive power when the Holy Spirit comes upon you, see Acts 1:8. Also in Mark 3:25, the Lord Jesus is saying that the house divided against itself cannot stand, so if you cast out a demon and you're a demon, it will not go away; that house will be divided. But if you cast it out by the finger of God it would tremble before you and leave. Why? Because the Lord Jesus and the Holy Spirit of the Living God dwell in your mortal body by the power of the Holy Spirit. That's God the Father's promise to the followers of His Son the Lord Jesus.

There **seems to be a reward for the righteous to work out their salvation with fear** (of God, a holy fear) **and trembling**—honouring God's eternal Word. See Philippians 2:12

Let me dig in here for us deeper: The Lord Jesus speaking in Matthew 7:24–25 said: *"Therefore everyone who hears these words of mine and puts them into practice is like a wise man who built his house on the rock. The rain came down, the streams rose, and the winds blew and beat against that house* (that house means your faith); *yet it did not fall, because it had its foundation on the rock.* The foundation is the Word of God. The Rock is Jesus. He remains and still is the Rock of our faith. The house that was battered by the storm (the problems we face in life) will stand because the foundation is solidly built on the Rock—the Lord Jesus and His teaching. You might say, "I really believe in the word of God." But do you put it into practice?

In verses 26 & 27 of Matthew 7 it says: *"But everyone who hears these words of mine and does not put them into practice* (*put into practice means there is work involved*) *is like a* ***foolish man*** *who built his house on the sand.* (Built himself up on people's common sense, not faith.) *The rain came down, the streams rose, and the winds blew and beat against that house, and it fell with a great crash."* When you build your house on the sand (sand means people—people's common sense, not faith in the Word of God), it will come crashing down with a bang! Putting into practice means to study the Word of God and asking God the Holy Spirit to enlighten the mind of your heart. Don't just believe what other people say. 2 Timothy 4:3 says: *For the time will come when people will not put up with sound doctrine. Instead, to suit their own desires,* ***they will gather around them a great number of teachers*** *to say what their itching ears want to hear.*

I consider the sand as the people, for in Genesis 22:15–17 it says: *The angel of the LORD called to Abraham from heaven a second time. and said, "I swear by myself, declares the LORD, that because you have done this and have not withheld your son, your only son* (you see Abraham did a work by acting on God's command and sacrificing his own son, see Genesis 22:1–14), *I will surely bless you and make your descendants as numerous as the stars in the sky and as* ***the sand on the seashore****."* When you build your house (faith) on the sand (people)—as a great numbers of teachers, and some born-again believers do—and not on the Word of God, your faith will suffer a big bang crash! The father of our faith did His work to make us believe, as did all the disciples.

And in Acts 19:13–16 we read: *Some Jews who went around driving out evil spirits tried to invoke the name of the Lord Jesus over those who were demon-possessed. They would say, "In the name of the Jesus whom Paul preaches, I command you to come out." Seven sons of Sceva, a Jewish chief priest, were doing this. One day the evil spirit answered them, "Jesus I know, and Paul I know about, but who are you?" Then the man who had the evil spirit jumped on them and overpowered them all. He gave them such a beating that they ran out of the house naked and bleeding.*

So you see you cannot cast out evil spirits if the Power of the Lord Jesus and the Holy Spirit is not operating in you. What I'm saying here is you cannot cast out demons if you have never been enlightened in your heart, mind and spirit by God's Power! In Matthew 7:21–23 we read: *"Not everyone who says to me, 'Lord, Lord,' will enter the kingdom of heaven, but only the one who does the will of my Father who is in heaven. Many will say to me on that day, 'Lord, Lord, did we not prophesy in your name and in your name drive out demons and in your name perform many miracles?' Then I will tell them plainly, 'I never knew you.'* Those people who were prophesying in the Lord's name and casting out evil spirits were all Christian believers, but why did the Lord Jesus say here that He never knew them? They practised lawless deeds, in God's sight, and since the Lord looks at the heart, God knew exactly what they were initiating in their hearts and minds. (You know when God made David, His servant, pay for his sin against Uriah, Bathsheba's husband—whom king David had killed by sending him to the front of the battle line and withdrawing from him—God considered David as a man after His own heart (though he sinned). God didn't kill David, but God killed his son to Bathsheba, and his own son Absalom fought against him. See 2 Samuel 12:11: *"Behold, I will raise up adversity against you from your own house."* So Absalom fought against David for sinning against God, and he died. David killed his own son through the battle of defending his kingship.)

The people in Matthew 7:21–23 are those counterfeit Christians. Maybe they are the ones whom the Lord called evildoers. 'Away from me, you evildoers!' I understand these verses sound like a warning to the believers. These people, as far as I know, are Christians (they are those who cast out demons and do miracles). But why would the Lord Jesus consider them as evildoers and say that He never knew them? If these people are true Christian believers, then surely they are saved!

And if we go even deeper in the scriptures we see here in Hebrews 6:4–6 that it says: *For it is impossible for those who were once enlightened, and have tasted the heavenly gift, and have become partakers of the Holy Spirit, and have tasted the good word of God and the powers of the age to come, **if they fall away, to renew them again to repentance, since they crucify again for themselves the Son of God, and put Him to an open shame.***

Does that mean that even believers could fall away from God? Well it says so! Some people think these passages mean that they will just lose their rewards in heaven and still be saved. Really, oh really? If you are crucifying the Son of God all over again and bringing a blaspheming spirit against the Son of God's final work, would you, a mere man, still expect to be saved? Ok, maybe not rewarded, but still saved? Unbelievable. Judgement is something to do with punishment, not rewards. While a reward is something to do with hearing the Lord say, "Well done good and faithful servant." You know then you will receive a reward.

If we move to 2 Peter 2:4–9: *For if God did not spare the angels who sinned, but cast them down to hell and delivered them into chains of darkness, to be* ***reserved for judgment****; and did not spare the ancient world, but saved Noah, one of eight people, a preacher of righteousness, bringing in the flood on the world of the ungodly; and turning the cities of Sodom and Gomorrah into ashes, condemned them to destruction, making them an example to those* ***who afterward would live ungodly****; and delivered righteous Lot, who was oppressed by the filthy conduct of the wicked (for that righteous man, dwelling among them, tormented his righteous soul from day to day by seeing and hearing their* ***lawless deeds)****—then the Lord knows how to deliver the godly out of temptations and to* ***reserve the unjust under punishment for the day of judgment****.* See also verses 10 & 11.

As for a lot of born-again Christian believers that think they could never lose their salvation—even if they do irretrievably wrong things, having a sloppy Christian walk with God at the end of their lives, and having known and experienced God's goodness and the Holy Spirit in their lives—their salvation would be wobbly and shaky!

If you're saying to yourself, "Well, I'm saved now, I can do everything I want and I wouldn't face any consequences, I'm saved," what a sloppy Christian you are. Is that reasoning acceptable in God's eyes? God put His only begotten Son to such an horrendous kind of death for us human beings, for our enormous sin. That was the Lord Jesus' purpose of His death. God the Father granted a once-and-for-all redemption for our sin. (Not to the dogs or cats or any other animals on earth, but to the people who have freedom of choice and the right mind.)

And in return would God the Father gain blasphemers, who exchanged the knowledge of God for a filthy, lawless living; ungrateful so-called born-again believers who exchanged the goodness of God for their fleshly lust and pleasure? Please read 2 Peter 2, the whole chapter.

When you have been enlightened by God and God the Spirit of the Lord Jesus, the Holy Spirit within you, and you choose to harden your heart and execute your fleshly ungodly desires, then **every time you do wrong in God's sight you blaspheme God, before the face of the devil**. Then the Lord Jesus will not even remember the good things you think you have done in the past, for you are giving the devil not just a foothold but the means to blaspheme God. For the Lord Jesus' complete and final sacrifice for all mankind has reached its finality. You or anybody else cannot crucify Him all over again and the LORD JESUS' WORD IS FINAL, when He breathed His last and declared, "IT IS FINISHED."

Why would GOD THE FATHER devalue what HIS SON HAS DONE ON THE CROSS, and gain you—a pathetic blasphemer, worm of the earth that he cast down with the devil to be judged? **What reward would you expect God to give you?**

What nonsense that you would even answer back to God? Do you really think you can even stand before God and talk back to Him? See Daniel 10:12–17. Daniel couldn't stand and was left breathless—and he was righteous in God's eyes; he was His true servant!

Moses was trembling with fear before the Angel of God, and he was considered to be seeing God face to face, and that he was a friend of God. That's how the Lord God revealed Himself to Abraham too. So who are you to stand before God and challenge Him?

1 Chronicles 21:30: *But David could not go before it to inquire of God, for he was afraid of the sword of the angel of the Lord.*

Luke 2:9: *And behold the angel of the Lord stood*

before them, and the glory of the Lord shone around them, and ***they were greatly afraid.***

The old prophets and people in the past could not stand before God, so who are you to throw an accusation before HIM?

There's this song that goes, I am a new creation, no more in condemnation, here in the grace of God I stand! In 2 Corinthians 5:17 it says: *Therefore, if anyone is in Christ, the new creation has come: The old has gone, the new has come.* And in Romans 8:1: *Therefore, there is now no condemnation for those who are in Christ Jesus.* Verse 3: *For what the law was powerless to do* ***because it was weakened by the flesh****, God did by sending his own Son in the likeness of sinful flesh to be a sin offering. And so He condemned sin in the flesh.* In contexts like this, the Greek word for flesh 'sarx' refers to the sinful state of human beings, often presented as a power in opposition to the Spirit. And in verses 5–7: *Those who live according to the flesh have their minds set on what the flesh desires;* ***but those who live in accordance with the Spirit have their minds set on what the Spirit desires. The mind governed by the flesh is death****, but the mind governed by the Spirit is life and peace. The mind governed by the flesh is hostile to God; it does not submit to God's law, nor can it do so.*

So the mind of the flesh and the mind of the spirit are contrary to each other. Unless the person in his or her freewill submits to the will of God, which is the Spirit of God, then they will not know God and be known by God. For God is a Spirit and not flesh. He who worships Him must come to Him in Spirit and in truth. (If you have accepted the Lord Jesus and you prefer to still walk in the suggestion of your flesh, then you are still away from God, since your own spirit doesn't want to cooperate with God's Holy Spirit.)

It's like having an absent father or mother. You know they're part of you, but you don't really know them because you never lived with them. Living with them means you developed a personal relationship, and you begin to know their traits, their likes and dislikes. You react, connect, joke and are cheeky with them, etc. But if they are not present in your everyday life, they know you exist, but they don't know you for who you are. Although it's difficult to compare a relationship with your parents and God's relationship with you, if you consider yourself a Christian, because in Christianity it's the Spirit form of relationship that counts—it's a higher cause, it's subject to God, it's reflective to Godly understanding, not looking inwards as to put yourself first. This is the spiritual Godly life! While the flesh life is always 'me first, you last,' 'I am better, you're not as good as me.' It's an inward focus, all in the flesh, as of a natural feeling and existence. There's no consideration for other's feelings, thoughts or needs—just me, I, myself and mine; so what? whatever! So relevant of today's lives: self-seeking, you have to like my way and what I feel, it has to be accepted. If I was born a girl and wanted to be a boy, you have to accept that I am a boy. But normal people that have been given Godly wisdom know the difference. And no-one should convince them what to believe.

There are those observers, and critics who venture on what they don't know about God's work. Some are believers in the first place, as they could do miracles and cast out demons in the Name of the Lord Jesus, so it means there are true Christian believers and there are counterfeit ones. If they can really cast out demons then they are true believers in Christ.

But wait a minute. It says in Hebrews 6:4–6: *It is impossible for those who have* <u>*once been enlightened,*</u>

who have tasted the heavenly gift, who have shared in the Holy Spirit, who have tasted the goodness of the word of God and the powers of the coming age and who have fallen away, to be brought back to repentance. ***To their loss*** *they are crucifying the Son of God all over again and subjecting him to public disgrace*. Have they lost their salvation at this crucial moment? How did they fall away? They have tasted the goodness of the Word of God and have shared in the Holy Spirit. **Are they still saved?** Can we really say, **Once saved, always saved?** How could you be still saved if you are crucifying the Lord Jesus all over again, and subjecting Him to public disgrace? Wow, surely not! This is the Word of God, not my word. When we Gentiles have tasted the power of the Word of God and the Holy Spirit, we are not exempted. Though it was written for the Israelites, we are engrafted and enlightened and became believers in Christ.

In Ezekiel 33:17–20: *"Yet your people say, 'The way of the Lord is not just.' But it is their way that is not just. If a righteous person turns from their righteousness and does evil, they will die for it. And if a wicked person turns away from their wickedness and does what is just and right, they will live by doing so. Yet you Israelites say, 'The way of the Lord is not just.'* ***But I will judge each of you according to your own ways.****"*

In Ezekiel 3:20: ***When a righteous person turns from their righteousness and does evil****, and* ***I*** *put a stumbling block before them,* ***they will die****. Since you did not warn them, they will die for their sin. The righteous things that person did will not be remembered, and I will hold you accountable for their blood.* (The LORD was talking to the prophet Ezekiel—he was known as a watcher of men.)

Ezekiel 18:24: *But if a righteous person turns from*

righteousness and commits sin and does the same detestable things the wicked person does, will they live? ***None of the righteous things that person has done will be remembered***. (This sounds like the Lord Jesus saying: *Then I will declare to them, I never knew you, depart from Me you who practice lawlessness*—Matthew 7:23.) *Because of the unfaithfulness they are guilty of and because of the sins they have committed, they will die.*

Ezekiel 18:26: *If a righteous person turns from their righteousness and commits sin, they will die for it; because of the sin they have committed they will die.*

These words the prophet declared did not originate from the prophet's mouths but originated from God. Otherwise he is a false prophet. But these are reliable prophets; their words are true and are from God. That's why they are all mentioned repeatedly. It strengthens the word of God for all believers.

Who then can be saved? Matthew 19:25–26: *When the disciples heard this, they were greatly astonished and asked, "Who then can be saved?" Jesus looked at them and said, "With man this is impossible, but with God all things are possible."* It's God's grace and mercy, with our cooperation. God cannot save you without your knowledge, the same as God cannot lead and guide and deal with you without your cooperation.

Matthew 7:15–20: *"**Watch out for false prophets.** They come to you in sheep's clothing, but inwardly they are ferocious wolves. By their fruit you will recognize them. Do people pick grapes from thornbushes, or figs from thistles? Likewise, every good tree bears good fruit, but a bad tree bears bad fruit. A good tree cannot bear bad fruit, and a bad tree cannot bear good fruit. Every tree that does not bear good fruit is cut down and thrown into the fire. Thus, by their fruit you will recognize them.*

I see it as this: You will see true Christian believers

and counterfeit ones. You will see them for who they are. True Christians rely on the leading and guidance of the Holy Spirit and the Word of God. And they put their faith into action according to the word of God and the continuing peace from the Holy Spirit. Not wanting to gain honour and wealth and popularity by using the name and the Word of God, but rather exposing the works of darkness, or the devil, and really upholding God in their hearts and in the midst of people who are sincere in serving God's purpose. <u>And it is always to build up people in the right way</u>, looking up to God as their Saviour, Lord and Father of their spirit man. They don't put their hope in the natural things they know of, and not in people either. Because whatever spiritual gift they have received—whether it's faith, prophecy, healing, etc.—they all came from God, and to the Only God shall praises and glory be, all praises and glory belong to God, not to them, for what they think they've done or achieved in life.

Hebrews 6:1–3 & 7–20: *Therefore let us move beyond the elementary teachings about Christ and be taken forward to maturity, not laying again the foundation of repentance from acts that lead to death, and of faith in God, instruction about cleansing rites, the laying on of hands, the resurrection of the dead, and eternal judgment. And God permitting, we will do so.*

Land that drinks in the rain often falling on it and that produces a crop useful to those for whom it is farmed receives the blessing of God. But land that produces thorns and thistles is worthless and is in danger of being cursed. In the end it will be burned. (People's work will be judged.)

Even though we speak like this, dear friends, we are convinced of better things in your case—the ***things that have to do with salvation. God is not unjust; he will not***

forget your work and the love you have shown him as you have helped his people and continue to help them. *We want each of you to* ***show this same diligence to the very end, so that what you hope for may be fully realized.*** *We do not want you to become lazy, but to imitate those who through faith and patience inherit what has been promised.* (Eternal life.)

When God made his promise to Abraham, since there was no one greater for him to swear by, He swore by Himself, saying, "I will surely bless you and give you many descendants." And so after waiting patiently, Abraham received what was promised.

People swear by someone greater than themselves, and the oath confirms what is said and puts an end to all argument. Because God wanted to make the unchanging nature of His purpose very clear to the heirs of what was promised, He confirmed it with an oath. God did this so that, by two unchangeable things in which it is impossible for God to lie, we who have fled to take hold of the hope set before us may be greatly encouraged. We have this hope as an anchor for the soul, firm and secure. It enters the inner sanctuary behind the curtain, where our forerunner, ***Jesus, has entered on our behalf****. He has become a high priest forever, in the order of Melchizedek.*

2 Corinthians 5:6–7 *Therefore we are always confident and know that <u>as long as we are at home in the body</u> we are away from the Lord. For we live by faith, not by sight.* Verse 10: ***For we must all appear before the judgement seat of Christ,*** *so that each of us may receive what is due us for the things done while in the body, whether good or bad.* (This, I believe, is something to do with rewards.) In verses 14 &15 it says: *For Christ's love compels us, because we are convinced that 'One died for all and therefore all died. And He*

died for all, THAT THOSE WHO LIVE SHOULD NO LONGER LIVE FOR THEMSELVES, but FOR HIM who DIED for them and was raised again.

Therefore, if anyone is in Christ, the new creation has come (that person now is a new creation): *the old has gone, the new is here!*—see 2 Corinthians 5:17. Some Christians say that if you are a true Christian you will not sin (you don't want to sin, and that is very true) because you love God. The fact is a lot of Christians love themselves. This is the truth: **you cannot love others if you don't love yourself.** But God loved us first while we were sinners, since God's love for us is unconditional. But we must also learn how to love God from our hearts. **Not because we know we truly love God, does God get any benefit from our loving Him.** No, not at all, we know that by loving God, we are benefited with His relational love for us. If we think we don't need God, then we don't need to respond to God's love. If we are all sufficient because we can do all things for ourselves, and we are determined to exclude God in our lives, then we make ourselves god of our own life. It means we're trying to show God that we can heal ourselves, and we can live without His intervention in our life; our life is our own decision and no-one else's. We're independent with no need of help from God. But if I say, "I love You today, Lord, because I need You to help me today," and tomorrow, "I'm not sure," and maybe on Sunday, "I love you again," that's changeable, inconsistent, and a most human kind of love. It's then based on what can I get, what benefit, what good is in it for me?

You can call on Him day or night and He will answer your prayer, when you make Him the God of your life. But if you're saying I love God, when your intention is just to benefit yourself, it means you are satisfied with yourself; you don't need God or anyone, just you the selfish one.

But when you understand the Lord's love and calling for you, He will begin to draw you close to Himself, but if you're so focused on your own emotions, He will allow you to make your own choice, out of your own freewill. He could continue to draw you close or leave you with your own consequences.

2 Peter 2:9: *Then the Lord knows how to deliver the godly out of temptations and to reserve the unjust under punishment for the day of judgement.*

Romans 4:2: *If, in fact, Abraham was justified by works, he had something to boast about—but not before God.*—SOMETHING TO DO WITH REWARDS.

2 John 1:8: *Watch out that you do not lose what we have worked for, but that you may be rewarded fully.*

Scriptures Based On Shaky Salvation For Lawless Unbelieving People.

Ephesians 4:18: *They are darkened in their understanding and separated from the life of God because of the ignorance that is in them* ***due to the hardening of their hearts.***

1 Corinthians 3:15: *If it is burned up* (as you work out your salvation), *the builder will suffer loss but yet will be saved—even though only as one escaping through the flames.*

2 Peter 2:20–22: *If they have escaped the corruption of the world by knowing our Lord and Saviour Jesus Christ and are again entangled in it and are overcome,* ***they are worse off at the end than they were at the beginning****. It would have been better for them not to have known the* *way of righteousness, than to have known it and then* ***to turn their backs on the sacred command*** *that was passed on to them. Of them the proverbs are true: "A dog returns to its vomit," and, "A sow that is washed returns to her wallowing in the mud."*

Hebrews 6:4–6: *It is impossible for those who have once been enlightened, who have tasted the heavenly gift, who have shared in the Holy Spirit, who have tasted the goodness of the word of God and the powers of the coming age and who have fallen away, to be brought back to repentance. To their loss they are crucifying the Son of God all over again and subjecting him to public disgrace.*

When we know that we are saved and that we are actually and totally walking according to the will of the Spirit of the Living God, then no-one can snatch us out of the Father's hand (and there's no need for anyone to be snatched away from God's hand), see John 10:28–29. But if we harden our hearts, then we fall away, otherwise these passages wouldn't need to be written for (us) believers, but as we read in Matthew 7:21–23: *"Not everyone who says to Me, 'Lord, Lord,' shall enter the kingdom of heaven, but he who does the will of My Father in heaven.* (What is the will of the Father? To believe in the One He sent, that is the Lord Jesus) You might say you believe. Excellent! Well done! The devil believes too, and shudders—see James 2:19. Let's continue with verses 22 & 23: *Many will say to Me in that day, 'Lord, Lord, have we not prophesied in Your name, cast out demons in Your name, and done many wonders in Your name?'* ***And then I will declare to them, 'I never knew you; depart from Me, you who practice lawlessness!'*** Does that mean you can or will still be able to practise lawless acts in front of God, after you have accepted Him in your life? I think the correct answer there is yes.

It also says in Philippians 2:12: *Continue to work out your salvation with fear and trembling.* Does that mean you still need to work out your salvation? Does that mean we have a part to play and do to protect or perfect? Thinking about it, yes; because we still have freewill and God will never take that away from us. So I believe so, answering my own question, otherwise it would just say, "You're saved now, sit back and relax."

For me it's obvious that they are losing their salvation. For only the crucifixion of the Lord, His sufferings on the Cross, and the resurrection from the dead will bring us salvation, and not rewards. Who are you to get a reward when you are trying to crucify the Saviour again? Who alone can save you through His Crucifixion? He gave us opportunity to have the free gift of eternal life.

In 2 Peter 2:20–22 this is what it says: *If they have escaped the corruption of the world by knowing our Lord and Saviour Jesus Christ* ***and are again entangled in it*** *and are overcome, they are worse off at the end than they were at the beginning. <u>It would have been better for them not to have known the way of righteousness</u>, than to have known it and then to turn their backs on the sacred command that was passed on to them. Of them the proverbs are true: "A dog returns to its vomit," and, "A sow that is washed returns to her wallowing in the mud."*

So it means there are those people who would go back to their old ways and old sins intentionally and be punished for their conduct. Yes, salvation is free and you do not have to work for it. But in the application of that salvation you need to do work, good work. As it says, *faith without works is dead*, so you still need to work; not for your salvation, but for the continued leading and guidance of the Holy Spirit in your everyday life, to keep your salvation.

In Hebrews 2:1–4 it says: *Therefore we must give the more earnest heed to the things we have heard, lest we drift away. For if the word spoken through angels proved steadfast, and every transgression and disobedience received a just reward,* ***how shall we escape if we neglect so great a salvation,*** *which at the first began to be spoken by the Lord, and was confirmed to us by those who heard Him, God also bearing witness both with signs and wonders, with various miracles, and gifts of the Holy Spirit, according to His own will?*

Hebrews 3:3–6: *For this One has been counted worthy of more glory than Moses, inasmuch as He who built the house has more honour than the house. For every house is built by someone, but He who built all things is God. And Moses indeed was faithful in all His house as a servant, for a testimony of those things which would be spoken afterward,* ***but Christ as a Son over His own house, whose house we are*** *if we hold fast the confidence and the rejoicing of the hope firm to the end.*

The reason we have been offered salvation is to enter the rest the Lord Jesus meant for us to have. You might think that equating rest with salvation is untrue or controversial. But without salvation you wouldn't have rest for your soul and spirit. Hebrews 4:9 & 10: *There remains therefore a rest for the people of God. For he who has entered His rest has himself also ceased from his works as God did from His.* You would have a continual warfare with enemy if you have never allowed God's Holy Spirit to claim you for God's sake (but actually for your own soul's sake). Entering God's rest means having peace with God. Peace means wholeness or completeness in God's Authority.

Hebrews 4:14–16: *Seeing then that we have a great High Priest who has passed through the heavens, Jesus the Son of God, let us hold fast our confession.* ***For we do not have a High Priest who cannot sympathize with our weaknesses****, but was in all points tempted as we are, yet without sin. Let us therefore come boldly to the throne of grace, that we may obtain mercy and find grace to help in time of need.*

12

REMEMBERING THE LORD JESUS' SACRIFICE

If we don't take communion, we are forsaking God's command **to remember Him**. We call it the breaking of bread. As Christians, we are commanded to **remember the Lord's body that was broken for us and His blood that was shed for us**, as His sacrificial love for the whole humanity, but especially for those people who believe in Him. It says in 1 Corinthians 11:23–31: *For I* (Paul) *received from the Lord what I also passed on to you: The Lord Jesus, on the night he was betrayed, took bread, and when he had given thanks, he broke it and said, "This is my body, which is for you; do this in remembrance of me." In the same way, after supper he took the cup, saying, "This cup is the new covenant in my blood;* ***do this, whenever you drink it, in remembrance of me****." For whenever you eat this bread and drink this cup, you proclaim the Lord's death until he comes.*

So then, whoever eats the bread or drinks the cup of the Lord in an unworthy manner will be guilty of sinning against the body and blood of the Lord. Everyone ought to examine themselves before they eat of the bread and drink from the cup. For those who eat and drink without discerning the body of Christ eat and drink judgment on themselves. That is why many among you are weak and sick, and a number of you have fallen asleep. But if we were more discerning with regard to ourselves, we would not come under such judgment.

I want to start with...*Everyone ought to examine*

themselves before taking communion; it means to check what's in your heart's attitude towards the people around you, for it would reflect your attitude towards the Lord Jesus. When the Lord Jesus said, *"Love your neighbour as yourself,"* it means you make your attitude acceptable before God. **The very thoughts of your heart are exposed to God**. If we could only remember first these words that Jesus said, *"Father, forgive them, for they know not what they are doing."* He called to God and extended His heart of forgiveness to those who crucified Him, on that cruel Cross. If the Lord forgave those who killed Him; we too ought to forgive those who hurt us, especially before taking communion. For in this it would expose what's in your heart.

By examining ourselves (before the Lord) we will be so aware of WHO we are remembering. Are we truly recognising and remembering what the Lord Jesus has done for us? The debt we owe to Him for obeying God Himself. The Lord Jesus paid in full **our inherited sin**, **for He knew we could never pay Him back**, or even come close to God. We cannot say, "It wasn't I who sinned, but it was those in the Garden." Let me remind you that without them, you wouldn't be here. It shouldn't be, "Oh I know He died for me"—head knowledge—but what is your heart knowledge of Him? Is your attitude acceptable or pleasing to God?

The Lord Jesus' forgiveness for His perpetrators came from His heart, not from His head. If you don't see it yet, it was all of us who put Him on the Cross!

Maybe you are feeling so hurt right now and you just could not forgive the people who hurt you, or abandoned you. And you've got a question, "Why, why do I have to forgive, why is it me, it's not my fault! O, Lord, why, why didn't You rescue me, Lord? Where were You? I thought you said You loved me? And right now I feel so desperate to hurt him or her back, just to let them know and feel what they made me feel, then and now."

It wasn't the Lord's will for you to be in pain and sorrow, and to have anger, hurt or bitterness. I want to let you know that God's intention for you is always good. **But this free will that people obtained from knowing good and evil is undoing God's whole power over you**, because God wouldn't cross over your will. If God had executed judgement on all humanity who sinned, not one person would be left on earth. But God loves all people, whether they are good or bad. If you're thinking this whole situation falls on humans alone and there's no enemy (the devil) behind all these bad events and wrong doing that people do to other people, then all humans have no need of rescuing—if we have power equal with the devil and his little demons. The Lord Jesus then did not need to die for you and me.

We hurt people and we point our fingers at people who have sinned against us. But since we can all now distinguish between good and evil, of course we are responsible for our actions. But the main point I'm trying to explain here is **the devil plays a massive part in fooling us to hurt others**, since our senses were triggered by the devil from birth, for we inherited sins that sweep through humanity, and by this we became self-centred.

God fights the battle for us through His Son's sacrifice fairly and justly. The devil was more powerful than human beings, and God knew that; He couldn't allow people to fight the battle alone when **the Lord Jesus knew that every time we fought, we would lose**. But after the Lord Jesus' death and resurrection, He gave us the power to fight the devil, more than equally with him, for the Lord Jesus fought the devil and won.

We're holding on to this knowledge; all we need to

know is who we are fighting against, and what tools are available for us. We fight not against flesh and blood—not physically—but we now fight against principalities and powers—through the Victory the Lord Jesus won on the Cross over that old devil. We claim Jesus' victory against the enemy by the power of His name and the power of His blood. As believers we've been given the permission to use Jesus' power against the enemy!

It says in Luke 10:19: ***I*** (Jesus the Lord speaking) ***have given*** (past tense) ***you*** (to all Jesus' disciples, and now all believers) ***authority to trample on snakes and scorpions*** *and to overcome all the power of the enemy; nothing will harm you.* You can only trample on things below you; **therefore God made you higher than the devil**. And it says in John 17:2: *For You* (that's Father God) *granted Him* (the Lord Jesus) *authority over all people* (us) *that He* (the Lord Jesus) *might give eternal life to all those You* (God) *have given Him* (the Lord Jesus).

The Lord wants us to see that it's the devil who is responsible for working havoc in people's lives. You have to understand that although it's people that hurt us, behind all these bad things that are happening it's actually the devil using people against people. Most ordinary people don't want to hurt others. But everyone has a choice to make, whether to do good or bad, and a lot of people work for their own advantage, for selfish gain or for their own gratification, that's the nature of man.

If you are so drawn to that pain at this moment, please do not take communion. But if you want to release yourself from that hurt and every awful emotion that goes with it, and you feel you can do so, forgive them; so you can be released from those hurtful memories. Please do this: close your eyes and say, "Lord

Jesus, please forgive me and let Your Holy Spirit overshadow me, I pray right now. Lord Jesus cover me and set me free from all this pain, neglect, abandonment, rejection, mental torment, and fear," and so on. Whatever you might be feeling, you need to give everything you're feeling to the Lord Jesus right now. "I give You my pain, Lord Jesus." (I know it's not easy.)

Maybe the person who hurt you is already dead, and you know you cannot hurt him or her back right now. But you are still aching because you are alive and hurting, and you are still suffering from those painful memories, and you can never erase them from your mind and your heart, because you were wounded so deeply. You only hear or say something and it triggers your pain over and over again.

Kneel down before the Lord, and ask the Lord Jesus to forgive all your sins first, though you are in pain. Say Lord, "Help me to receive Your healing!" Ask for God's healing and compassion to fall on you first, to make you whole from the inside.

Maybe you're thinking you need a break from all these hurts and pain and regrets. If from your heart you have this burden of constant rejection and pain, let me encourage you: the Lord Jesus looks at the heart and He can see your heart right now; He is ready to help you.

So for those who are hurting, please say this, "Lord Jesus help me to have a rest in my soul from this pain. Please, Lord Jesus, take away from me all these hurts I'm carrying. I would like to put them down, and the only place I could dump them is at the foot of Your Cross. Refresh me, O God, and enable me to forgive my perpetrators. Forgive all my sins, Lord, that I may able to forgive these people." Mention their names one by one the—the Lord Jesus knows all of them. (He gave life to them.)

Then say this: "Bring healing to my soul, O My Saviour, that You may forgive me; and that I may be able to forgive others, that You may release me, Lord Jesus, from this pain I'm suffering from. Help me, O Lord My God and precious God the Holy Spirit.

If all you have is pain, that's all you can give—pain to others. **YOU CANNOT GIVE WHAT YOU HAVEN'T GOT**. That's why you need the Lord Jesus to forgive you first, so that you can forgive others their sins. Now you've been forgiven (or keep it to yourself till you're ready, the Lord will help you), you can now extend forgiveness to those who hurt you, for you have now got the forgiving spirit the Lord Jesus placed in your heart. You will now be able to forgive others, because you have received that forgiving spirit from the Lord Jesus, if you get what I mean!

I feel I need to be real here, for you cannot forgive anyone if you're in tremendous pain yourself. As I said earlier, start gossiping to the Lord Jesus about the person who hurt you. Then ask God's forgiveness for yourself first, for holding on to your perpetrator's pain (I know it's difficult to process these things in our normal brain cells), so that you may receive God's spiritual forgiveness in your heart and soul. So after you receive the Lord Jesus' forgiveness, you can now extend the grace of being forgiven by God, to forgive those who hurt you.

And if you cannot forgive yet, please, please, do not take any communion at this time, so you don't sin against the memory of the Lord Jesus' sacred sacrifice.

Receive God's healing first and forgiveness, so that you may extend to him or her what you received from the Lord Jesus.

Are you holding some sort of displeasure towards others, are you brewing anger or jealousy in your heart?

Do you feel any rejection by some of your family members, colleagues or friends? Or do reject yourself, thinking other people invalidate me? It's normal to have negative thoughts of yourself—it's the nature of men. But don't let that nature disqualify you from feeling whole and at peace again.

So first of all, you've got to forgive the people who have hurt you, and ask the Lord to forgive you for sitting in that pain you are suffering from.

Somebody said that hurting people hurt others. If you think you've hurt somebody, admit it to yourself that you are in the wrong, before God, and then to others, if necessary. Your own pride wouldn't choke you, but you will be released from that guilty feeling, so that you may have peace in your heart, and your guilty conscience will be cleansed.

The enemy (that's the devil) attacks us from our thoughts, then our emotions follow as we entertain those feelings from what our minds dictate. It reaches the heart and we become angry and bitter, and sometimes it locks a person to some sort of illness. Why? because the pain in our minds and emotions are heavy things to carry in our soul; it truly is exhausting! Even if you're normally a happy kind of person and you don't get easily offended, there will be times when you get annoyed with other drivers on your way to church, and you might swear in your head. Release and forgive that person who cut you up. For it says in Romans 12:2: *Do not be conformed to this world, **but be transformed by the renewing of your mind, that you may prove what is that good and acceptable and perfect will of God.*** Also, in Ephesians 4:23–24 it says: *and be renewed in the spirit of your mind, and that you put on the new man, which was created according to God, in true righteousness and holiness.* To renew your mind is to set your mind on things above, not on things on the earth. And in Colossians 3:12–14: *Therefore, as God's chosen people, holy and dearly loved, clothe yourselves with compassion, kindness, humility, gentleness and patience. Bear with each other and forgive one another if any of you has a grievance against someone. Forgive as the Lord forgave you. And over all these virtues put on love, which binds them all together in perfect unity.*

We must examine our hearts to see if there is any offensive way in the sight of God in us—things you're ashamed to expose to the Lord. Bring them to light, ask for the Lord's forgiveness and leave it to the Lord. God knows the heart and mind of all people, so if you can speak to someone who hurt you or someone you hurt, speak to them. They might be aware of what you've done to them. Say sorry to them, do it, but don't go running after them, if you think they are not aware of what they did to you. Just between you and God, ask for His peace within you, and the Holy Spirit's presence which is alive in you will then heal you; that is your confidence in Him. You know He heard you and has forgiven you. But you have to **remember forgiveness is not a feeling, it's a decision you make.**

Know He has already forgiven you the minute you acknowledge your sin before Him. If the person you've hurt is close by to speak to, go and speak to them and be reconciled to them. So that your motive is acceptable to God and He would accept you. That's the first step to examining yourself.

"For those who eat and drink without discerning the body of Christ ***eat and drink judgement on themselves.***—that is a heavy word—*That is why many among you are weak and sick and a number of you have fallen asleep*, see 1 Corinthians 11:29–30. I see it as this: if you take the communion in an unworthy manner, you

may die!

So do not take communion when you have a feeling of unforgiveness or jealousy or anger or any other negative feeling towards someone. Ask God to forgive your attitude and forgive the person you're feeling so bad with, **so you don't eat and drink judgement on yourself**.

After examining yourself, and having forgiven all who have sinned against you and whom you have sinned against, you can now go on to the next stage which represents the healing for you and others who believe that by the Lord Jesus' stripes (wounds) you are healed, see Isaiah 53:5 and 1 Peter 2:24: *Who Himself bore our sins in His own body on the tree, that we, having died to sins, might live for righteousness—by whose stripes you were healed.*

The righteousness of the Lord Jesus, which brings righteousness to us, could now bring healing to us too, as we ponder in our hearts that only through His sacrifice can we be healed. No other remedy but through the righteous and powerful blood of the Lord Jesus, can we claim not only salvation, but also healing for others—and yes, for ourselves too.

There should be seriousness in taking part of the body and blood of Jesus Christ of Nazareth, as you are partaking of that meal, for the Lord Himself said, "Remember Me whenever you take this bread"—representing His broken body as His sacrifice for you—"and drink My blood"—which is the cup of the Lord Jesus' sufferings for us. It's no joke and not a laughing matter.

Some people are not taking seriously the breaking of bread (which represents both salvation and healing for those who believe). Even some ministers would comment, "Oh, this bread is a bit chewy," or "This cracker is a bit crunchy," or "This juice is a bit sour," etc. It means if you are commenting on such things, you are not really serious in part taking of God's Holy communion which was and is His Son's blood that would cleanse you from your sin, and His body which is broken for you—in which you claim healing from!

I would like to say, shame on you, for taking Him as a joke. It's better not to take communion than to take it and insult His whole sacrifice, by your own attitude. Your head knowledge attitude of remembering what is written in the Bible will bring you nothing. It should be sincere, and should be from your heart's recognition of what He did for you. **So be aware that when God's Son was hanging on the Cross He was not joking!** That's the only way you can have salvation (and you have to work out your salvation) and that's also the only way we can be close to Him and receive our healing. When He told His disciples to **"Remember Me,"** He meant do it with gratitude and reverence, not taking it for granted. It was a SACRED MEAL between the Lord Jesus and His disciples. We're continuing, and so don't do it without due respect for Him!

You might be able to even memorise what it says in the Bible about His Words, but it won't do you any good if you don't take it seriously, and you just laugh when you're doing it. Rude—shame on you! Let me say, if the queen or some person with authority offered you bread that was a bit dry, you wouldn't say to her face, "This is a bit dry," just to break the ice, would you? So why say it when taking communion?

How can you receive healing when you have just laughed at His sacrificial death on the Cross? Because when it comes to the truth, you caused Him His own death. Why would the Lord Jesus himself listen to you, when you ask for healing, when you have just insulted his finished work on the cross? Why would God the Father and the Holy Spirit even come near or even look at you with compassion when you have just insulted Him? I know He's not a God or man that easily gets offended, but it's like sticking your tongue out at the Lord Jesus, then saying, "Heal me!" Why would He listen to you? He would laugh at you. The Lord laughs at those people who scoff at Him, see Psalm 2:4–5 and Psalm 37:13.

How very dare you insult the Lord Jesus Christ's complete sacrifice! You may insist that you didn't laugh at His sacrifice and death, but you laughed when you chewed on the crackers or dry bread which represents His body, and you commented on the juice that represents His blood. Why does it have to be during the remembrance time that you laugh and make a comment about that juice and that bread that you are eating?

Maybe that's why some people who take communion in an unworthy manner become sick and ill and die because of it, see 1 Corinthians 11:27 & 29–30.

Do not take communion if you're not serious about it. Don't take it just because you know how to do it, or just for the sake of doing it. For there is a consequence if you don't take seriously the Lord Jesus' sacrifice and His death on the Cross for you. This is a warning.

13

DO YOU KNOW WHERE YOUR SPIRIT IS GOING TO WHEN YOU DIE?

Have you ever asked yourself what the meaning of life is, and what really happens when we have achieved everything we want to achieve in life? Would I truly get satisfaction and fulfilment in life, be at peace within myself and be happy? Or would I still be hankering after new achievements in life?

Where does life end? I know it's not after retirement. Is it after we die? If someone dies receiving everything they aimed for in life, will they be happy in death? And what's going to happen with all my wealth that I worked so hard for? I know I cannot take it with me when I die. Is this all what life is about? Have you ever wondered if death is the finality of everything, including life itself?

Do you really know where you are going to after your body is in the ground, six foot under, and you don't have hope in death as well as life? You may think, "But I'm dead; where is there to go to, but to the earth and rot there forever, my bones only popping up now and again if someone digs me up accidentally?" Would you still consider your carcass or bones as yourself? Could you still claim that the bones buried long ago still belonged to you? Think about it—who would be saying to you, "Oh, that, that bone was me." You might say, "I've never been there yet, how am I supposed to know?"

You know, all appliances when bought new have an instruction manual enclosed. Well, let me tell you the good news—we come with a manual for life too. Our manual is the Bible, but it's not just a manual, it is the food for our souls too, the living Word. Our everyday existence depends on it. You may think, "How could this be?" Well, the bible is the true food for our souls. All living beings have soul and spirit; if you don't have a spirit, you are dead. Death in the physical is the stop of all functions in the natural way of life.

You might say, "I am not Christian; I do not have the same values in life as them." But do you value yourself? Perhaps we Christians are focused on life after death, or life eternal, as we Christians call it. You may ask me what basis I've got for all these things. Look around you. When you know someone who has died, can they talk, can they move? Do you think they can think? You know, when the body is dead, the mind is dead too, right? So it means the thinking is outside the body, right? And that thinking outside of the body is the spirit of a person.

In Isaiah 46:9–10 it says: *I AM GOD, and there is no other; I Am God, and there is none like Me. I MAKE KNOWN THE END FROM THE BEGINNING, from ancient times, what is still to come.*

I am the Lord, the Maker of all things, who stretches out the heavens, who spreads out the earth by myself—Isaiah 44:24.

I AM the Lord and there is no other; apart from Me there is no God. I form the light and create darkness, I bring prosperity and create disaster; I, the Lord, do all these things—see Isaiah 45:5 & 7.

You might say, "What has it got to do with me?" Well, you are living on the earth that God so beautifully created, and you are alive because He breathed the breath of life into your spirit, when He created you in your mother's womb.

It says in Psalm 139:14: *I will praise You for I am fearfully and wonderfully made; Marvellous are Your works, and that my soul knows very well.* (The heading in the NKJV version of this Bible chapter reads: God's perfect knowledge of Man.) Verses 15–17: *My frame was not hidden from You, when I was made in secret, and skilfully wrought in the lowest parts of the earth. Your eyes saw my substance, being yet unformed. And in Your book they were all written* (there is a book of life in heaven, see Revelation 20:12) *the days fashioned for me, when as yet there where none of them. How precious also are Your thoughts to me, O God! How great is the sum of them!* It wasn't man's presumed knowledge, but it's God's perfect knowledge of man.

Every person born is known by God. How true it is that there is a time to be born and a time to die, and that there is a time in every season under heaven, see Ecclesiastes 3. The Bible also says in John 3:7: *"You must be born again,"* and it never came from a human ideology, but directly from the Lord Jesus who was and is the author of life itself. The author of all creation.

The Lord Jesus knows your beginning and your end. Sometimes we think we know, and we think that God doesn't know, and if God does know, we have always a question. How come that you /we say, "God loves me/you and yet He allowed this to happen, or let so and so die in such and such circumstances? Why is there famine and all the bad events happening in the lives of people?" I believe sometimes He wants to let us (inhabitants of the whole earth) know who is God and who is not! If God gave us a freedom of choice, I do believe **GOD has that freedom of choice too**; to do what He needs to do for His Creation. After all, the heavens and earth belong to Him! Who would argue with God to say differently?

God's love does not consist of what we think in the natural. We always cater for the good of our own self, relatives, friends and so forth and so on, but God—being all-powerful and all-loving—does not have the same mind as we humans have. His thoughts are higher than our thoughts and His ways are higher than our ways, see Isaiah 55:8–9. Can you really argue with God, who even gives the breath of life in your very life? He created the air we breathe. Without air we cannot breathe. If we could only stop and think how marvellous are God's love, care, sufferings and dedication for His creation, and even the ability He indulged us with. What we see, hear, touch, taste and smell all come from Him. Our own observation of nature is all created by Him, the Lord Jesus, for Him, and through Him. Without the Lord Jesus' participation with God the Father, nothing would exist in heaven and on earth, see John 1:3–4.

I see it as this: The Lord Jesus was with God in the beginning of creation (His name was the Word) see Genesis 1:26 and John 1:1–2. The Lord Jesus agreed in the first place for Father God's creation to take place. If the Lord Jesus hadn't agreed, Father God could not have sent anyone on God's behalf. Remember, He said that *He could only do the work He sees the Father doing*, see John 5:19.

Now with the tree of life and the tree of good and evil, which were the testing objects by God to man, we have obtained knowledge through our freewill. **Without freewill we couldn't be tested, because we wouldn't be able to disobey God.** We would be like robots that would just go and do all the assignments God wanted us to do. But the Lord didn't see that as love; that binds people to servitude. God wants us to have freedom, just like the angels God created, and the fallen angels too had freedom. And due to the Lord Jesus' agreement of creating man, He carried on His Shoulders the responsibility of redeeming us. That's why the Lord Jesus is and was the Only One who has the power to redeem and rescue us from the enemy's grasp.

The Lord Jesus alone has the power to do that, for no-one else could agree to purchase all people by His Holy blood. Father God, Lord Jesus and the Holy Spirit, all agreed to do this in the first place. So here we see the Father sent the Son, and the Holy Spirit guided and strengthened the Son's Heart and helped Him to finish the Sacrifice. The Lord Jesus our Creator is the Only One who could save human creation from the curse of death, brought about because of the disobedience of the first human beings on earth, when they disobeyed God's commands (exercising their freewill).

But there was a choice that was hidden from the devil when he instituted for man to sin, when he incited them to eat from the tree of the knowledge of good and evil. If human hands had touched the Tree of Life, the disobedience would be complete; we would be thoroughly doomed to die spiritually forever. God knew that when Adam and Eve acquired the knowledge of good and evil, they would be redeemable through the Lord Jesus' sufferings on the cross.

In the book of Revelation, chapter 19, verse 7 and Revelation 21, verses 2 & 9, we know the church (Christian believers) is the bride of the Lamb (Christ is known as the Lamb of God, John 1:29). See also Revelation 22:17. Before the fall, Adam and Eve's relationship with the Almighty God was hunky dory. But after the humans sinned, the Lord Jesus put Himself up to pay the dowry for His bride, the Church—the would-be believing body of Christ. For the Lord Jesus to redeem all human males and females—if they are willing—God the Father sent the dowry, His Co-Creator of heavens and earth. So the Lord Jesus needed to die (His death is His dowry).

It is mentioned in the Gospels that unless a seed dies

it will only remain a single seed, but if it dies, it produces many more seeds, see John 12:24. His death cost such a high price for God the Father, whether people believe Him or not. But since millions of people now believe in His death, we are the seeds that sprouted from the one Seed that died, when we became believers of Him, through God's word. But for all the unbelievers I can only say they still need Christ, whether they know or agree, or not, for God's Words is the Ultimate Unchanged Power in the heavens and on the earth. So if you're on earth, you've been warned!

God really will judge all creation, see 2 Timothy 4:1. According to this verse, the living and the dead will be judged, at the Lord Jesus' appearing the second time. The first time He came as a baby in the manger, He grew up and showed us His Love, His mercy, His power and His ways through the disciples and His teaching. He came then just to love, not to judge the world but to condemn the sin (but not the sinners) of the world through His death and resurrection.

But the second time He comes back (whether you believe it or not) the Lord Jesus will pronounce judgement on all the inhabitants of the earth, and condemn the sinners that did not repent of their sins. For all have sinned and fall short of the glory of God, see Romans 3:22–24.

The second coming is near, so make sure you are not included in those people who will be judged. If you're saying, "How could I go from here to there?" the simple answer is: if you repent and believe in His death and resurrection, then the justice of the Lord will come as your defence. But if you're trying to say to yourself, "How could I believe in the one I don't know and see or hear?" then may I take the pleasure of telling you that life and time are short, but as long as you have breath in your nostrils then you are not yet too late. If you are saying, "I cannot force myself to believe that all these things about Jesus are true," then ask the Lord yourself: "Is it true, Lord Jesus, that if I don't repent and accept You, acknowledge You, here on earth, You will not acknowledge me at the throne of God, and judge me instead when I die?"

I mean, it's your soul and spirit that will be judged, not your physical body, because only your flesh will be rotting in the earth. Your spirit and your soul (which feels the pain and every emotion here while we are on earth) will live forever and be judged. But if you say, "Lord, I'm a sinner; You are righteous, save my spirit and my soul from the judgement that will come against everyone who is now living (and also those who are already dead); lead me, please, and guide me to Your truth, save me, O God, that I may be saved," then you will not be judged.

If you're saying, "Why would I listen to you, Naylee, and you other people who told me about this Jesus as Lord over my soul, body and spirit?" then read the Bible.

If you're saying to yourself, "I'm an atheist, that's my religion; I don't believe," still you can never ever evade the requirement of the Lord to know Him and your soul to be recognised and reconnect with Him. Because the very breath you are breathing today is from Him. You would never be on this earth if you didn't agree from your mother's womb to be born, and to come and live as you are unless approved by Him in the first place. Yes, God gave you freedom of choice, but if you are wise enough you would choose Him, who owns the land, the sea, the sky and all the inhabitants of the earth, for He created it as we see it today, see Psalm 24:1–3. And in John 1:1–3, it says: *In the beginning was **the Word**, and **the Word** was with God, **and the Word was***

***God**. He was in the beginning with God. All things were made through Him, and without Him nothing was made that was made.* And who is the Word? The Word is Jesus.

In Genesis 1:26 it says: *"Let Us make man in Our image, according to Our likeness."* So Jesus was there at the beginning of creation. God spoke the Word and the world was created. And the Holy Spirit was there, hovering over the surface of the deep (Genesis 1:2) when the God of all mankind created everything. See also Colossians 1:16–18.

Let me tell you what the Lord Jesus said in John 3:1–21:

There was a man of the Pharisees named Nicodemus, a ruler of the Jews. This man came to Jesus by night and said to Him, "Rabbi, we know that You are a teacher come from God; for no one can do these signs that You do unless God is with him."

Jesus answered and said to him, "Most assuredly, I say to you, unless one is born again, he cannot see the kingdom of God."

Nicodemus said to Him, "How can a man be born when he is old? Can he enter a second time into his mother's womb and be born?"

Jesus answered, "Most assuredly, I say to you, unless one is born of water and the Spirit, he cannot enter the kingdom of God. That which is born of the flesh is flesh, and that which is born of the Spirit is spirit. Do not marvel that I said to you, 'You must be born again.' The wind blows where it wishes, and you hear the sound of it, but cannot tell where it comes from and where it goes. So is everyone who is born of the Spirit."

Nicodemus answered and said to Him, "How can these things be?"

Jesus answered and said to him, "Are you the teacher

of Israel, and do not know these things? Most assuredly, I say to you, We speak what We know and testify what We have seen, and you do not receive Our witness. If I have told you earthly things and you do not believe, how will you believe if I tell you heavenly things? ***No one has ascended to heaven but He who came down from heaven, that is, the Son of Man*** *who is in heaven. And as Moses lifted up the serpent in the wilderness, even so must the Son of Man be lifted up, that whoever believes in Him should not perish but have eternal life. For God so loved the world that He gave His only begotten Son, that whoever believes in Him should not perish but have everlasting life. For God did not send His Son into the world to condemn the world, but that the world through Him might be saved.*

"He who believes in Him is not condemned; but he who does not believe is condemned already, because he has not believed in the name of the only begotten Son of God. And this is the condemnation, that the light has come into the world, and men loved darkness rather than light, because their deeds were evil. For everyone practising evil hates the light and does not come to the light, lest his deeds should be exposed. But he who does the truth comes to the light, that his deeds may be clearly seen, that they have been done in God."

You may ask why we Christians are always banging on about Jesus. It's because we cannot help telling you all about the truth. Jesus said, *"I am the way the truth and the life, no man comes to the Father* (that's our God) *except through Me* (John 14:6). God never tells lies, only ever the truth. (The author of lies is the devil, and he is the accuser of the brethren—fellow Christians and others.)

Everything was made through Jesus; dominion and power and might are from Him. *For by Him all things were created that are in heaven and that are on earth, visible and invisible, whether thrones or dominions or principalities or powers. All things were created through Him and for Him. And He is before all things, and in Him all things consist. And He is the head of the body, the church, who is the beginning, the firstborn from the dead, that in all things He may have the preeminence.* (Colossians 1:16–18.)

People come and go but no-one has ever said or testified to have come back to life and died on a cross for the sin of the world. And if there is someone claiming this, as the Lord Jesus has been claiming from the beginning of the world, he or she will only be copying—it will be counterfeit. Thank God no-one has ever claimed that yet, but at the end of time it will be seen that only Jesus has the answer, the true answer.

What have we Christians achieved if all we do is let you atheists know about the power of God over you all? Maybe received an insult, mocking, saying we don't have a brain, we believe in the air, in something that's not there, that doesn't exist. But I'm telling you, if one day you die and you wake up in hell and you cannot leave the place, what are you going to do? Blame the Christians, because they didn't warn you? Surely you cannot blame yourself because you know everything! The Bible is just a book of airy-fairy stories, made up from Christian people's bad imaginations.

So if one day you wake up in hell, you have been warned by a Christian—so there! I have taken my responsibility of telling you about eternal life in heaven, and hell too, even if it's only from this book. When you have been warned and you don't take heed, your own blood is on your head!

14

DID YOU KNOW GOD HAS A SENSE OF HUMOUR?

Once I was telling the Lord how good He is to me and I probably kept on repeating it much more than I intended to, because I heard the Lord say, "You're getting mellow dramatic." And I don't really know what I was thinking at that time, but I know God looks at the heart. What was in my heart at that time, I'm not sure, I can't remember, but God knows.

Now there was a Christian lady who told me a story of a mother who accidentally locked her baby inside her brand-new car, and her house keys with it. (If you remember those kinds of car that can be locked by pushing the button inside, and once you've slammed the door closed the car is locked.) This lady who locked her baby inside the car was a new Christian believer. After realising what she had done, as she couldn't get inside the house to phone for help and her baby was crying and hungry, she couldn't do anything but pray. In her prayer she said, "Lord, I'm praying please, **Lord, please, send me please a professional car thief** who could open my car door without damaging it. Upset and annoyed with herself, she carried on praying.

A few minutes later a man was passing by, he saw her crying and approached her by asking, "Why are you upset and crying?" Sobbing, she replied, "I've locked my keys in my car, and I can't take my baby out and she's hungry, she needs feeding; I can't go in my house as my door key is inside my car. I'm so stupid, I'm so stupid, and I don't know what to do."

This man felt so sorry for her and said, "Don't worry lady," he reassured her, "I will help you open your car and get your baby out."

"What have you got to hand to use?" Everything she suggested didn't help. Eventually the man spotted a long rigid plastic tape lying around on the ground, the one used for tying up parcel boxes. He reluctantly picked it up and pushed it through a little gap in the car window, hooking the door knob with a loop, and pulled up the lock button, managing to open the car door in seconds. He retrieved the car keys and she got the crying baby out of the car and thanked the man.

She couldn't stop thanking him. She said, "You're a very, very, good man; you're just like an angel to me.

"No, lady, I'm a bad man. I'm a very, very, bad man!"

Frowning, the lady insisted. "You just helped me open my car door to get my baby out of my car. You're a very, very, good man!"

The man replied, "Lady, I really am a bad man; I just came out of prison today. I was put in prison for thieving cars; **I was a professional car thief.** And I became a born-again Christian when I was in the jail. I promised God that if He would help me to get out of prison, I would do my best to work honestly to earn a living with my hands. I don't want to carry on living with tainted hands. And this is my first day out of prison.

"When I saw you, I was contemplating between visiting my parents and going to the hostel accommodation. When I saw you crying and your baby crying locked inside the car, I didn't really want to help, I just wanted to carry on walking. But when I saw your baby crying, face red and so upset inside the car, I couldn't just pass by; I felt the Lord wanted me to help you. I carried on walking but I felt disturbed in my heart, as I know I could help you. I was so reluctant to use this plastic tape; I knew I could open your car in seconds with it, as that's the only tool I used to keep in my pockets to steal cars. But I want a new life now. I want to use my hands to do good work for a living. I don't want to be a car thief any more."

The lady remembered her prayers and said to the man, "I am a new Christian too, and when I couldn't get to my baby inside my car, **I prayed, 'Lord, please, please Lord, send me a professional car thief**, so that my car would not be damaged, and help me, please; take my baby out of the car. So the Lord sent you to me."

The man scratched his head, and said, "God answered your prayers." The lady had a little giggle to herself and invited him in her house to give him something to eat, but he refused. So she handed him some cash, and before going on his way, he thanked her and said, "I still want to get a proper job."

I could see that God has definitely got a sense of humour. Thank You Lord.

www.ingramcontent.com/pod-product-compliance
Lightning Source LLC
LaVergne TN
LVHW010924110826
845149LV00013B/2469

* 9 7 8 0 9 9 5 6 8 2 3 2 0 *